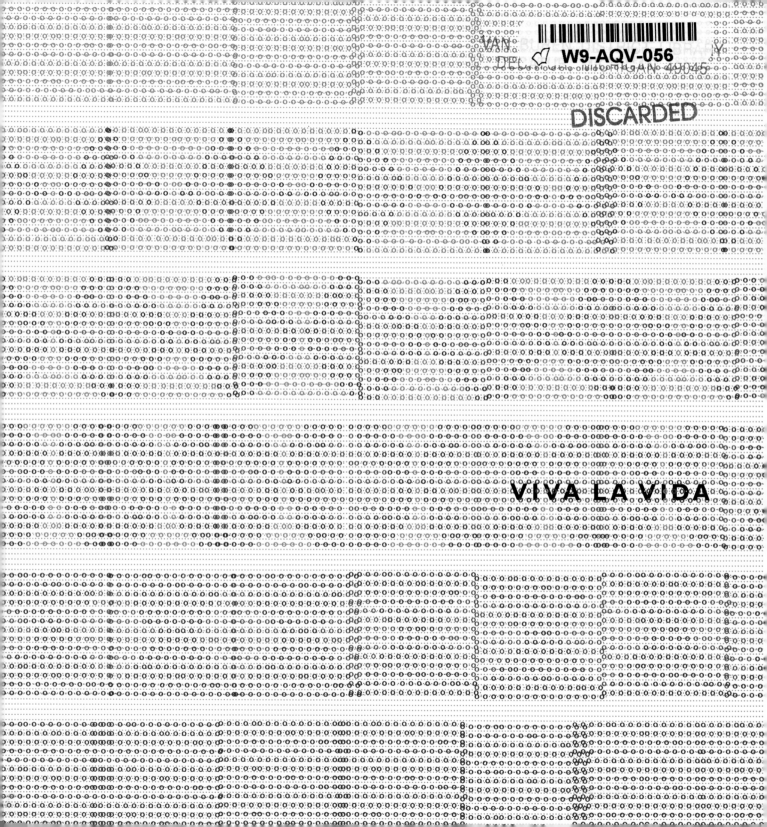

VIVA LA VIDA

VIVA LA VIDA

FESTIVE RECIPES FOR ENTERTAINING LATIN-STYLE
BY RAFAEL PALOMINO AND ARLEN GARGAGLIANO
PHOTOGRAPHS BY SUSIE CUSHNER

CHRONICLE BOOKS
SAN FRANCISCO

Library of Congress Cataloging-in-Publication Data:

Palomino, Rafael, 1963–
    Viva la vida : festive recipes for entertaining Latin-style / by Rafael Palomino and
Arlen Gargagliano ; photographs by Susie Cushner.
    p. cm.
    Includes index.
    ISBN 0-8118-3184-1 (pbk.)
    Cookery, Latin American. 2. Entertaining. I. Gargagliano, Arlen. II. Title.
    TX716.A1 P355 2002
    641.598—dc21
    2001028816

Manufactured in China.
Prop styling by Sara Slavin
Food styling by Sandra Cook
Designed by Elixir Design
The photographer wishes to thank Sara Schneider for graciously providing the opportunity for me to bring a group of experienced, like-minded creators together who committed and worked tirelessly in an atmosphere of perfect interaction, fun, and focus. Sara Slavin brought refined mastery of style, along with her beautiful nature. Sandra Cook, a food stylist extraordinaire, is relentlessly organized and tireless. My deep appreciation and gratitude to both for moving this project forward. I am also grateful for the incredibly hard work and perfect assistance from Jon Kishimoto. To Gina Cere, Alex and Johnathan Edward, and Mark and Sara for support during the invasion.

Distributed in Canada by Raincoast Books
9050 Shaughnessy Street
Vancouver, BC V6P 6E5

10 9 8 7 6 5 4 3 2 1

Chronicle Books LLC
85 Second Street
San Francisco, California 94105
www.chroniclebooks.com

DEDICATION

I dedicate this book with love to Martha, my wife, to Amanda, my daughter, and to Rafael, my son.

—Rafael Palomino

I dedicate this book with love to my husband, Seth Markusfeld, whose support and patience I couldn't live without; my children, Sofia and Wes, who fill my life with joy, wonderment, and laughter; my parents, Sonia and Tony Gargagliano, who made me believe that I could do anything I set my heart on; and Rafael, whose love of food—and life—is contagious.

—Arlen Gargagliano

ACKNOWLEDGMENTS

Many thanks to:

My writer, Arlen Gargagliano

My great, great agent, Jane Dystel (without her, this book wouldn't have been done!),

My editor Bill LeBlond, along with Amy Treadwell, and the staff at Chronicle Books,

My managing staff at Sonora: Oscar Galvan, Ivan Cepeda, Angela María Jaramillo, Angel Jurio, Moe Gad, and my chef de cuisine, Jorge Peña,

My kitchen–, wait–, and bar staff at Sonora,

Larry Forgione, for being a mentor and friend, and

John Mariani.

I would also like to thank my mom, Graciela Palomino, and my dad, Rafael Palomino. Thanks also to my sister, Gloria Moreno, and my brother and financial partner, Martin Palomino. And lastly, thanks to my little niece Laura, who always helps me in the kitchen, and who is on her way to being part of the next generation of Latina chefs.

CONTENTS

CHAPTER THREE **SIDE DISHES**

CHAPTER FOUR **MAIN DISHES**

INTRODUCTION

Fresh *maracuyá*, or passion fruit, dances with just-squeezed lemons in a glistening glass pitcher. Cilantro leaves scatter through my fingers, along with garlic and chopped tomatoes, to a sizzling finish in hot oil. I quickly stir the *ají*, or Colombian salsa, in the small sauté pan on our action-packed stove. My father, large fork in hand, smiles "*Ya está el lechón*" ("The roast suckling pig is ready"), as he lifts it out of the oven. My mother unveils the steaming stack of freshly roasted *arepas*, or Colombian corn cakes, just enough to send the sweet roasted-corn aroma wafting through the bustling kitchen, then wraps them delicately in a napkin as she heads toward the dining room. Platters of roasted chorizo, Colombian sausage, and *tostones*, or golden brown coins of fried green banana, already grace the tables set for our usual Sunday extended-family gathering. The soft, soothing voice of Carlos Vives (a Colombian folksinger) serenades us as my father lifts up his glass of wine in a toast: "*Salud, amor y dinero, y tiempo para gozar los tres*" ("Health, love, and money, and time to enjoy all three")

It is this weekend ritual, filled with food, family, and fun, that I want to share with you; this is what Latin-American parties are all about. Our fiestas celebrate life on a daily basis. A fiesta is a family dinner, a small informal get-together with a few friends, an elegant meal for several guests, or a large, wild party with the whole neighborhood! The sparkle is in the company—no matter how small or large—and in the spirit of the *comida*, or food.

Growing up in Bogotá, family gatherings were an integral part of my life. My cousins and uncles—as well as neighbors and their relatives—shared many week-ends of eating, laughing, drinking, and enjoying life together. These memories of love and food, eternally intertwined in *la cultura latina*, Latin culture, makes me want to give my own family—in a new country and a new time—the same rich memories.

My parents raised me to enjoy the process as much as the product. Trips to the market, like Bogotá's famous Siete de Agosto, were adventures that never ceased to dazzle. Winding through a labyrinth of vendors, *mis hermanos y yo* (my brother, sister, and I) would joke with the sellers who called for our mother to buy from them. My mother, driven by impulse rather than a prepared list, would scan the displays prior to engaging in extended conversations with the vendors. We would follow, munching on little *galletas* (cookies), chunks of cheese, and other samples the vendors would hand us. We felt welcome, comfortable, and connected.

I sometimes liken those markets to a marriage between Fairway, a great New York City supermarket, and Balducci's, one of the same city's finest gourmet markets, simply because you could find just about anything there: fabulous assortments of cheese, just-baked breads, piles of fruit whose colors and arrangements delighted the eye, freshly prepared *batidas* (fruit shakes), fresh herbs and spices, vegetables, dried beans, and an incredible assortment of meats, poultry, and fish.

On our return home, my mother would give us specific tasks: husking corn, chopping cilantro, cutting avocados and tomatoes, and of course setting the table. While we prepared, we talked about everything from what was going on in school to political events and gossip. The joint preparation of our fiestas made us feel—from a very young age—that we were a part of just about everything. This sense of community is what defines my culture.

My roots reach deep into the heart of Latin America. Though I feel Colombian first and foremost, I also feel a part of all that is Latino. Being Latino means sharing part of the traditions of that area we call Latin America, which stretches approximately seven thousand miles from the top of Mexico down to the tip of Cape Horn in Argentina and includes twenty-two different countries. Gorgeous sandy beaches, expansive deserts, lush rain forests, and snow-capped majestic mountains are just some of the area's physical features. Needless to say, this incredible variety of climatic, topographic, and geographical attributes leads to a greatly diverse assortment of cuisines. Even within my own native Colombia we have an enormous wealth of foods, ranging from Caribbean fish and cooling African-influenced coconut dishes, found along the coast, to Spanish-influenced warming *estofados*, or stews, found in the cooler mountainous regions. Of course, the *rasgos*, or roots, of our own indigenous peoples are visible still, as they are all over Latin America, in the primary foods of the *Nuevo Mundo,* or New World: beans, corn, chilies, and squash. Nevertheless, our sharing is not just culinary, but also cultural: We share a passion for *vida,* or life. This passion is shown through our sense of family, community, and our outlook on life.

Today, my wife and I continue the tradition of the *fiesta latina:* We love to keep our house filled with family, love, and laughter—and of course, great food. We strive to give our children the rich *ambiente,* or environment, that we were raised in.

Since my wife and I started throwing parties at home more than twelve years ago, we've been greeted with accolades from our friends and family members. And the best part is that my wife and I enjoy the parties as well! So, what makes our fiestas such fun? Our parties are planned around two fundamental hosting principles: first, that we are able to remove ourselves from the kitchen and enjoy the party, and second, that pre-party stress be kept to a minimum thanks to careful planning. This book was written to give you a *mano*, or a helping hand, so that you can achieve the same success with your own parties.

The recipes in this book, which are written in simple, step-by-step instructions, are the result of my life and experiences; I've combined aspects of my Colombian heritage, my French culinary education, my New York experience, and most recently the nuevo Latino cooking of my New York City restaurant, Sonora, in order to bring you dishes that are exciting, easy to prepare, delectable, and beautiful. Even if this book is the one that introduces you to the world of Latin-American cooking, you will be able to enjoy the preparation, the serving—and of course the consuming—of these dishes.

Viva la Vida welcomes you to a world of cooking that promises to be the beginning of a great culinary *aventura*, or adventure, for you. You'll find a wide variety of dishes, including succulent salsas and dips, exciting appetizers and side dishes, dazzling main dishes, delectable desserts, and luscious drinks to accompany them all. Though most of the ingredients are easily accessible, I've also provided a list of mail-order sources.

I encourage you to turn the pages of this book and start cooking! Get to know my recipes. Find your favorites and share them with your family and friends. And who knows? After some time you may even begin experimenting and adding your own *toques*, or touches, to these dishes. Remember, the most important part is *disfrutar*: to enjoy!

SALSAS AND DIPS

SALSA ROJA

This simple sauce is as good on a grilled steak or a nice piece of Chilean sea bass as it is as a dipping sauce for chips. Have all the ingredients prepared prior to the arrival of your guests, then toss the salsa together as drinks are being served. The smoky flavor of the chipotle is distinct but not overpowering. MAKES ABOUT 5 CUPS

6 plum tomatoes, finely diced

2 small red onions, finely diced

2 cups tomato juice

1/4 cup chopped fresh cilantro

1/4 cup distilled white vinegar

1 tablespoon Chipotle Purée (page 174)

Freshly ground pepper to taste

In a large bowl, combine the tomatoes, onions, tomato juice, and cilantro. Stir well, using your hands or a wooden spoon. Add the vinegar, chipotle purée, and pepper. Stir again. Serve immediately, or cover and refrigerate for up to 3 days.

ARGENTINE PESTO (CHIMICHURRI)

If I had to be stranded on a desert island with only one salsa, this would be it. This is just one of my versions of the classic Argentine pesto. My kitchen always has *chimichurri* on hand. At the restaurant, we call it the South American barbecue sauce. Whether it's for marinating meat and shrimp, grilling portobello mushrooms, or simply for spreading on fresh crusty bread, *chimichurri* is an excellent complement to many foods. To make a sun-dried tomato variation, simply add 5 coarsely chopped oil-packed sun-dried tomatoes prior to blending. (Or, soak dry-packed tomatoes in warm water to soften before adding.) MAKES ABOUT 2 CUPS

4 cloves garlic, coarsely chopped

1 1/4 cups loosely packed fresh cilantro leaves

1 1/2 cups olive oil

Kosher salt to taste

Freshly ground pepper to taste

1 1/2 tablespoons fresh lemon juice

3/4 cup white balsamic vinegar

2 green onions, including light green parts, thinly sliced

In a blender or food processor, combine all the ingredients and process to a smooth sauce. Use now, or cover and refrigerate for up to 1 week. Stir well before serving.

BLACK BEAN AND CUMIN DIP

Cumin adds a rich, toasted flavor to these hearty black beans, while the chipotle adds bite! Depending on your taste, you may want to add more chipotle purée. MAKES ABOUT 2 1/2 CUPS

3 cups cooked black beans (page 175), broth reserved

2 teaspoons ground cumin

4 teaspoons Chipotle Purée (page 174)

2 tablespoons tahini (sesame paste)

Kosher salt and freshly ground pepper to taste

In a blender, combine the beans, cumin, chipotle purée, and tahini and process to a smooth sauce, adding the reserved broth or water as needed. Add salt and pepper. Serve now, or cover and refrigerate for up to 5 days.

TRADITIONAL FRESH COLOMBIAN SAUCE (AJÍ COLOMBIANO)

Ají is as important to the Colombians as *chimichurri* is to the Argentines. Hardly a meal in my home is served without this clean-tasting Colombian condiment. We enjoy scooping it up with crusty meat-filled empanadas, Malanga Chips (page 40), or Yuca Fries (page 76), and we also spoon it over grilled fish and steak. This rich salsa varies according to region. My version, which is heavily influenced by my native city, Bogotá, combines beefsteak tomatoes, green onions, cilantro, and the whites of hard-cooked eggs. MAKES ABOUT 4 CUPS

4 green onions, including light green parts, thinly sliced

2 large beefsteak tomatoes, seeded and diced

1 1/2 red onions, finely diced

1 bunch cilantro, stemmed and chopped

7 hard-cooked egg whites, chopped

2 tablespoons chopped fresh chives

3/4 cup olive oil

1 teaspoon Tabasco sauce

1/3 cup white wine vinegar

Juice of 1 fresh lime

Kosher salt and freshly ground pepper to taste

In a large bowl, combine the green onions, tomatoes, and red onions. Stir to blend. Add the cilantro, egg whites, and chives. Stir to blend. Gradually stir in the olive oil. Add the Tabasco, vinegar, lime juice, salt, and pepper. Stir to blend. Serve now, or cover and refrigerate for up to 2 days.

BASIC COLOMBIAN SAUCE (SALSA CRIOLLA)

Much like the ubiquitous bottles of ketchup on U.S. family tables, *salsa criolla* is kept on hand in my family to blanket grilled meat, chicken, fish, and vegetables. MAKES ABOUT 3 CUPS

- 2 tablespoons olive oil
- 1 red onion, thinly sliced
- 2 cloves garlic, minced
- 1 teaspoon ground cumin
- 6 ripe plum tomatoes, cut lengthwise into strips (reserve juice and seeds)
- 2 cups chicken stock (page 180) or canned low-salt chicken broth
- Pinch of sazón spice blend (page 187)
- Kosher salt and freshly ground pepper to taste
- 8 Peruvian or niçoise olives, pitted and coarsely chopped
- ¼ cup coarsely chopped fresh cilantro

In a medium sauté pan or skillet, heat the oil over medium heat and sauté the onion and garlic for 3 minutes. Stir in the cumin, tomatoes, and reserved juice and seeds. Add the stock or broth, sazón, salt, and pepper. Simmer for several minutes. Stir in the olives and cilantro. Serve now, or cover and refrigerate for up to 2 days.

PERUVIAN THYME-NIÇOISE SAUCE

When I was nineteen years old, I spent an incredible year living in southern France and learning French cooking from the highly acclaimed French chef Michel Guérard. There, I learned how to combine foods and herbs to bring out the best in both. On returning to New York, I began to combine my new French-cooking knowledge with my Latin-American roots. This sauce has a lot of flexibility. I've served it with Crabmeat and Sweet Plantain Empanadas (page 50) as well as with Chimichurri Lamb Chops with Goat Cheese (page 110). I also like to drizzle it on top of roasted potatoes and fresh crusty bread. MAKES ABOUT 2 CUPS

Leaves from 1 handful fresh thyme

Leaves from 1 handful fresh rosemary

1½ cups olive oil

16 Peruvian or niçoise olives, pitted

2 cloves roasted garlic (page 184)

Cumin, kosher salt, and freshly ground pepper to taste

In a blender or food processor, combine the thyme, rosemary, olive oil, and olives. Add the garlic and blend until smooth. Add the cumin, salt, and pepper. Serve now, or cover and refrigerate for up to 1 week.

COLOMBIAN TOMATO SAUCE (SOFRITO)

Just as the French have their *mirepoix*, we have *sofrito*: a vegetable sauté used in many Latino dishes as a base or as topping. This sauce is always on hand in my home and in my restaurant. In this particular *sofrito*, the roasted garlic delicately embraces the sweet flavors of the tomato and onion. This sauce enlivens stews, soups, and beans; dresses up Yuca Fries (page 76); and adds a graceful finish to Sonora's Seafood and Chorizo Paella (page 103). MAKES ABOUT 1 1/2 CUPS

2 tablespoons olive oil

1 small onion, finely chopped

1 teaspoon roasted garlic (page 184)

3 tomatoes, cut into 1/4-inch dice

3/4 teaspoon sazón spice blend (page 187)

1/3 cup finely chopped green onions, including light green parts

1/3 cup chopped fresh cilantro leaves

1 bay leaf

1 cup chicken stock (page 180), canned low-salt chicken broth, or water

Kosher salt and freshly ground pepper to taste

Heat the oil in a medium, heavy saucepan over medium heat and sauté the onion and garlic for 1 minute. Add the tomatoes, sazón, and green onions. Sauté until the onion is translucent, about 2 minutes. Add all the remaining ingredients and simmer for 7 to 10 minutes. Use now, or let cool, cover, and refrigerate for up to 1 week. You can also freeze this sauce for up to 6 months and thaw just prior to using. Stir well before serving.

PALOMINO'S GUACAMOLE

These days it is not too hard to find this Mexican dip on grocers' shelves, but I urge you to make it yourself. Not only is it very simple to prepare, it's also *mucho mejor* (much better) when you make it at home. Guacamole is excellent party fare because its soft, rich flavor contrasts beautifully with many kinds of crunchy chips. (It's also great the next morning on a toasted bagel.) MAKES ABOUT 2 1/2 CUPS

4 ripe Hass avocados, peeled, pitted, and coarsely chopped

1 red onion, diced

1/4 cup chopped fresh cilantro

1 teaspoon Tabasco sauce

1 teaspoon kosher salt

2 red beefsteak tomatoes, finely diced

Juice of 1/2 lemon

In a large glass or ceramic bowl, combine the avocados, onion, and cilantro. Toss well; the avocado will get mushy. Add all the remaining ingredients and stir until well blended. Serve now or cover and refrigerate for up to 1 day.

MANGO AND LIME RELISH

Several years ago, I had the opportunity to spend time in Las Brisas, a fabulous hilltop hotel in Acapulco, Mexico. Every morning I enjoyed the sunshine and a platter of fresh mango, papaya, and pineapple, which I ate while admiring the breathtaking view of the Pacific Ocean. It is this sensual feeling of sun, fresh fruit, and ocean that I relive every time I eat grilled red snapper bathed with this mango relish. MAKES ABOUT 3 CUPS

1 mango, peeled, cut from pit, and cut into 1/4-inch dice

1 ounce (2 tablespoons) gold tequila

Juice of 1 orange

Juice of 2 limes

6 fresh mint leaves, stacked, rolled, and cut into fine shreds

2 tablespoons olive oil

1 teaspoon Pommery or Dijon mustard

1 cucumber, seeded and cut into 1/4-inch dice

Kosher salt and freshly ground pepper to taste

In a medium glass or ceramic bowl, combine the mango, tequila, orange and lime juices. Stir to blend. Add the mint leaves, olive oil, mustard, and cucumber. Add the salt and pepper and stir. Serve now, or cover and refrigerate for up to 3 days.

COLOMBIAN BRANDY CHUTNEY (CHUTNEY DE AGUARDIENTE)

I've always loved experimenting with different taste combinations. This chutney works well with everything from grilled burgers to fish. My wife enjoys it dolloped on top of a green salad in lieu of dressing. MAKES ABOUT 1 3/4 CUPS

2 mangos, peeled, cut from pit, and finely diced

Kosher salt and freshly ground pepper to taste

2 ounces (1/4 cup) aguardiente (Colombian brandy) or Greek ouzo

1 cup diced cucumber

2 tablespoons coarsely chopped fresh chives

1/2 cup mango nectar

1 lime, halved

Put the diced mango in a large bowl and add salt and pepper. Add the aguardiente or ouzo, cucumber, chives, and mango nectar. Use your hands or a spoon to stir the mixture until well blended. Squeeze the lime over, and mix again. Serve now, or cover and store in the refrigerator for up to 5 days.

PEAR AND CITRUS RELISH

This exotic cumin-kissed relish is good with fish, grilled chicken, and grilled chicken sausages. The mint and figs give this relish a Middle Eastern touch. MAKES ABOUT 4 CUPS

Juice of 3 oranges

5 Bartlett or Anjou pears, peeled, cored, and finely diced

10 figs, coarsely chopped

1 ounce aguardiente (Colombian brandy) or Greek ouzo

6 fresh mint leaves, rolled and cut into fine shreds

Pinch of ground cumin

1 tablespoon canola oil

1 tablespoon white wine vinegar

Kosher salt and freshly ground pepper to taste

In a medium saucepan, cook the orange juice over medium heat to reduce by half. Let cool to room temperature. Meanwhile, in a medium bowl, combine the pears, figs, aguardiente or ouzo, and mint leaves. Stir until well blended. Add the cumin, oil, vinegar, reduced orange juice, salt, and pepper. Serve now, or cover and refrigerate for up to 2 days.

APPETIZERS

ASIAN-GLAZED GRILLED QUAIL (CHINO-LATINO CODORNIZ A LA PLANCHA)

While visiting Peru, I was impressed by the Japanese and Peruvian fusion of ingredients and dishes. Years before, when I was a teenager, I was introduced to the world of sushi and sashimi and quickly became a fan. (Even today, I often crave tuna hand rolls and run to the nearest sushi restaurant!) The Japanese influence of clean, fresh flavors and aesthetically pleasing food arrangements marries well with my own version of Latino cooking. I started creating Asian-Latino dishes on the menu at Sonora (such as Ceviche Chino Latino, page 62, and Chino-Latino Tiradito, page 69). This dish of grilled quail has been a big hit both at home parties and in the restaurant. Serve it with Palomino's Rice with Beans (page 82). SERVES 6 TO 8

Marinade:

3/4 cup garlic oil

1/2 cup soy sauce

2 teaspoons chipotle purée (page 174)

1/2 cup honey

1/2 cup dry white wine

6 to 8 partially boned quail (about 5 1/2 ounces each), butterflied

Prepare an outdoor grill or heat a grill pan over high heat. In a large bowl, whisk all the marinade ingredients together. Rinse and wipe the quail dry inside and out with a paper towel. Add the quail to the bowl and toss to coat evenly. Grill the quail for about 2 1/2 minutes on each side, or until well browned on the outside and opaque throughout. Place on a serving platter or individual plates and serve immediately.

BLACK BEAN, CORN, AND SHRIMP QUESADILLAS

My guests at Sonora—and at home—eat these as soon as the platter appears! The beauty of these quesadillas is that you can play around with the filling depending on the availability of ingredients and your taste. Quesadillas can be conveniently prepared for unexpected guests (make sure you keep some ice-cold Coronas in the fridge). For parties, I serve quesadillas on a platter and decorate them with stripes of guacamole and sour cream, which I keep in handy, plastic squirt bottles.

SERVES 12

1 tablespoon olive oil

6 medium shrimp, shelled, deveined, and cut into $1/4$-inch dice

$1 1/2$ cups fresh or thawed frozen corn kernels

2 cups cooked black beans (page 175)

3 plum tomatoes, diced

1 cup chicken stock (page 180) or canned low-salt chicken broth

3 green onions, including light green parts, thinly sliced

$1/4$ teaspoon ground cumin

Six 8-inch-diameter flour tortillas

1 cup shredded Cheddar cheese

Preheat the oven to 350°F. In a medium sauté pan or skillet, heat the olive oil over medium heat and sauté the shrimp for about 3 minutes, or until pink on both sides. Add the corn, beans, and tomatoes. Stir in the stock or broth, green onions, and cumin. Stir and set aside.

Arrange the flour tortillas on a work surface. Divide the cheese evenly over them. Add the shrimp mixture and fold the tortillas into a half-moon shape. Place them on a baking sheet, and bake for 5 to 7 minutes, or until the cheese melts. *¡Tengan cuidado!* Be careful! You don't want the tortillas to get too crispy.

Cut the quesadillas in half, place them on a platter, and serve immediately.

MALANGA CHIPS

Whether it's at the bar at Sonora or in my home, malanga chips seem to disappear as soon as I put them out for guests. The nutty flavor of this tropical tuber gives these chips enough flavor to stand on their own, but I also like to serve them with ceviche. Malanga chips are also good to crumble and use as a coating, as in Sea Scallops with a Malanga Crust, page 87. Yuca or green plantains can be substituted for malanga in the following recipe. MAKES ABOUT 2 CUPS

1 1/2 pounds malanga, scrubbed and peeled

Peanut oil for deep-frying

Kosher salt for sprinkling

Using a mandoline, the slicing blade of a food processor, or a large chef's knife, cut the malanga into very thin lengthwise strips. In a heavy pot or deep fryer, heat 1 inch oil to 365°F. Working in batches, gently add malanga slices one at a time (otherwise they will stick together) to the hot oil and cook for 2 to 3 minutes, or until browned on both sides. Using a skimmer, transfer to paper towels to drain. Sprinkle with salt and let cool. Serve now, or store in an airtight container for up to 5 days.

ECUADORIAN SHRIMP WITH A CHIPOTLE-CITRUS MARINADE

This is a great summertime party dish because it is cooked outside and requires virtually no prep time. My guests especially enjoy this treat when served along with Passion Fruit Margaritas (page 162) and Mashed Plantains and Potatoes (page 94). SERVES 6

18 medium shrimp, shelled (some like to keep the tail on for easy grabbing) and deveined

1 tablespoon garlic oil (page 183)

Kosher salt and freshly ground pepper to taste

1 teaspoon chipotle purée (page 174)

Juice from 6 oranges

Juice from 3 limes

Arrange the shrimp in one layer in a shallow bowl. Lightly coat the shrimp with garlic oil. Add salt and pepper. Dab the shrimp with the chipotle purée (squeeze bottles are great for this). Pour the orange and lime juices over the shrimp, and turn them over to coat them well. Let sit for at least $1/2$ hour or a maximum of 1 hour.

Prepare an outdoor grill or use a grill pan. Drain the shrimp, reserving the marinade. In a small saucepan, bring the marinade to a boil and cook for 5 minutes. Heat the grill pan, if using, over high heat. Oil a perforated grill rack or the grill pan. Arrange the shrimp on the grill or in the pan and brush the marinade on top. Let cook for about 2 minutes, or until pink on the bottom, then turn and recoat with marinade. Cook just until pink on the second side, about 2 more minutes. Transfer to a large platter and serve immediately.

ARGENTINE BEEF SKEWERS (ANTICUCHOS DE CARNE DE ARGENTINA)

Whether they're called *pinchos*, as in Colombia, or *anticuchos*, as in Peru, skewered beef is a popular Latin-American treat. One of my first stops in Lima, Peru, is always Las Tejas, in Miraflores, where I enjoy sitting outside with old friends, drinking ice-cold *chelas* (beer), and munching on freshly grilled *anticuchos de corazón*, beef-heart skewers. This adaptation of *chimichurri*-blanketed anticuchos, made from Argentine rib-eye steak, is popular with family and customers at Sonora. *Anticuchos* are easy to prepare, incredibly tasty, and great to serve at any get-together. For larger groups, simply place them on a large, centrally located platter, next to a cooler of chilled Cuzqueñas (Peruvian beer)—or any beer—and let your guests help themselves. MAKES 6 SKEWERS

8 ounces Argentine rib-eye steak, trimmed of fat and cut crosswise into six 4-inch-long, 1/2-inch-thick slices

Kosher salt to taste

1/2 cup Argentine Pesto (page 21)

Soak six 8-inch wooden skewers in water for 30 minutes; drain. Prepare an outdoor grill, or heat a grill pan over high heat. Oil the grids or pan.

Thread each slice of meat lengthwise on a skewer. Sprinkle with salt. Use a brush or your fingers to coat each piece of skewered meat with the *chimichurri*. Grill for about 3 minutes on each side for medium-rare meat, or according to desired doneness.

CHILEAN SALMON TARTARE ROLLS

One of the beauties of salmon is that it is so easily married with other flavors. This roll is an elegant brunch appetizer, ideally served with Mango and Lemongrass Sangría (page 161) or Passion Fruit Margaritas (page 162). MAKES 8 ROLLS

1 pound very fresh Chilean or American salmon fillets, pin bones and skin removed

½ red onion, finely chopped

2 tablespoons Chipotle Mayonnaise (page 174)

½ Hass avocado, peeled, pitted, and cubed

½ teaspoon minced fresh chives

Juice of ½ lime

Kosher salt and freshly ground pepper to taste

Four 8-inch-diameter flour tortillas

1 tablespoon crème fraîche or sour cream for garnish

With a sharp knife, cut the salmon into $1/4$-inch dice. Put the salmon in a large bowl. Add the onion and chipotle mayonnaise and mix gently. Add the avocado, chives, and lime juice. Stir just until blended. Add salt and pepper and stir again. Place a tortilla on a work surface and spread about 3 tablespoons of the salmon mixture over it. Tightly roll up the tortilla. Repeat with the remaining tortillas and filling. Cut the rolls in half and stand them up on a platter. Using a squirt bottle filled with crème fraîche or sour cream, garnish and serve.

YUCA PASTELES STUFFED WITH ARGENTINE SIRLOIN STEAK

The beauty of this appetizer is that you can make these *pasteles* ahead of time and freeze them. For more guests, simply multiply the amounts. Serve them next to bowls of salsas or *ají* so guests can drizzle them with the sauce of their choice. MAKES 2 PASTELES; SERVES 4

Filling:

1 teaspoon oil

1 cup 1/4-inch-diced sirloin steak

1 red onion, finely diced

1 teaspoon sazón spice blend (page 187)

3 tablespoons thinly sliced green onions, including light green parts

1 small zucchini, coarsely chopped (optional)

1/2 cooked carrot, coarsely chopped (optional)

Kosher salt and freshly ground pepper to taste

2 hard-cooked eggs, coarsely chopped

Dough:

1 pound yuca, peeled, cooked, and cut into 1/2-inch dice (page 186)

3 cups chicken stock (page 180) or canned low-salt chicken broth

1/2 cup dried bread crumbs

Canola oil for deep-frying

Mixed salad greens for garnish

Salsa Roja (page 20) or Palomino's Guacamole (page 29), optional

To make the filling: In a medium sauté pan or skillet, heat the oil over medium heat and sauté the sirloin and onion for 3 minutes, or until the sirloin is springy to the touch. Add the sazón, green onions, optional zucchini and carrot, salt, and pepper. Sauté, stirring frequently for 3 to 5 minutes, or until softened. Remove from heat and transfer to a medium bowl. Add the eggs and mix just until blended.

To make the dough: In a large saucepan, combine the yuca and stock or broth. Bring to a boil, reduce heat to medium, cover, and cook for about 10 minutes, or until the yuca is tender. Remove from heat, drain the yuca, and put it in a large bowl. Whisk or mash the yuca to the consistency of mashed potatoes. Add the bread crumbs and mix well. The mixture should be slightly sticky and elastic.

Cover a work surface with a sheet of plastic wrap. Place half of the dough on the plastic wrap and cover with another sheet of plastic. Using a rolling pin, roll the dough out to an 1/8-inch thickness. Remove the top piece of plastic and spread half of the filling over the dough. Roll the dough into the shape of a large egg roll about 8 inches long and fold in the ends. Repeat with the remaining dough and filling.

In a deep, heavy pot or deep fryer, heat 2 inches of oil to 365°F. Fry the *pasteles* one at a time until browned, about 4 minutes. Using tongs, transfer to paper towels to drain. Keep warm in a preheated 250°F oven for up to 20 minutes if necessary.

To serve, cut each roll in half on the diagonal and place them standing up on platters garnished with mixed salad greens. Serve plain, or with salsa roja or guacamole, if you like.

SEARED SEA SCALLOPS ON CORN TORTILLAS WITH AJÍ VERDE

When I was a little boy, my mother often played matchmaker for singles in our neighborhood. She'd invite prospective mates to join our family gatherings. Curiously, she would often serve "messy" food on these occasions so that, according to her philosophy, *todos estarían más tranquilos*, everyone would be more relaxed. While I'm not quite sure if this philosophy works for matchmaking, it certainly is fun to be able to scoop up food. This appetizer is one to be devoured, as the contrast of meaty scallops and crunchy tortillas definitely puts this appetizer in the tasty and messy category. Serve the remaining *ají verde*, a simple and tasty typical Colombian sauce, with additional tortillas or Malanga Chips (page 40). SERVES 6 TO 8

1 tablespoon canola oil

4 corn tortillas

12 sea scallops

Ají Verde:

2 avocados, peeled, pitted, and sliced

Kosher salt to taste

1/4 cup finely chopped red onion

1/2 teaspoon chipotle purée (page 174)

1/4 cup finely diced mango

Juice of 1 fresh lime

Preheat the oven to 350°F. In a large skillet, heat the oil over high heat. Cut the tortillas into quarters and fry for 1 to 2 minutes, or until crisp. Using a slotted spoon, transfer to paper towels to drain.

Add the sea scallops to the pan and sear until browned on each side, about 3 minutes total. Immediately place the scallops on a baking sheet and bake for another 3 minutes. (Don't overcook, or they'll be like rubber!) Remove from the oven and set aside.

To make the *ají*: In a medium bowl, mash the avocados. Add the salt, onion, and chipotle purée and stir well. Add the mango and squeeze lime juice on top. Stir to blend.

Top each corn tortilla with 1 teaspoon of the *ají verde*. Top with a scallop and then just a touch of *ají*. Repeat until you've used up the tortillas and scallops. Serve immediately.

CRABMEAT AND SWEET PLANTAIN EMPANADAS

Ripe plantains are a must for this dish, which will have your guests begging for more. Pass these treats around as your guests enjoy their first cocktails. Empanadas are great appetizers, because you can prepare them ahead of time. You can even buy empanada leaves (Goya makes them) and skip the dough-making step. Serve with Peruvian Thyme-Niçoise Sauce (page 25), or naked (I mean, without any sauce)! MAKES ABOUT 22 EMPANADAS

Dough:

1 tablespoon garlic oil (page 183)

5 cups precooked cornmeal (*harina precocida*)

3 cups hot water

1 teaspoon kosher salt

Freshly ground pepper to taste

Filling:

1 teaspoon unsalted butter

2 very ripe (black) plantains, peeled and cut into $1/2$-inch dice

1 pound fresh lump crabmeat

2 tablespoons Chipotle Mayonnaise (page 174)

1 teaspoon Peruvian Thyme-Niçoise Sauce (page 25)

Canola oil for deep-frying

To make the dough: In a small saucepan, heat the garlic oil over medium heat. Put the cornmeal in a large bowl and add the hot garlic oil. Pour in the hot water and stir. Stir in the salt and pepper. Using your fingers, mix the *masa*—dough—until it's elastic, about 4 minutes. Cover and refrigerate for 10 minutes.

To make the filling: In a medium sauté pan or skillet, melt the butter over medium heat. Add the plantain chunks and sauté until browned. Remove from heat. Put the crabmeat in a large bowl. Stir in the plantains, chipotle mayonnaise, and thyme-niçoise sauce. Set aside.

Cover a work surface with a sheet of plastic wrap. Remove the dough from the refrigerator, place it on top of the wrap, and cover it with an additional sheet of plastic. Using a rolling pin, roll the dough out to an 1/8-inch thickness Then, keeping the plastic wrap on top, use a 2 1/2-inch biscuit or cookie cutter to cut out rounds of dough.

Take off the top layer of plastic wrap and remove the dough between the rounds; set aside. Place 1 heaping teaspoon of filling on the bottom half of each round. Use the plastic wrap to fold each circle over. Seal the edge with your moistened finger. Repeat for each empanada. Reroll the remaining dough and make additional empanadas until you've used up the filling.

In a deep, heavy pot or deep fryer, heat 2 to 3 inches oil to 365°F. Fry the empanadas, a few at a time, until golden and puffed. Using a skimmer, transfer to a wire rack set on a baking sheet. Serve immediately, or let cool, then freeze for up to 3 months. To reheat, bake on a baking sheet in a preheated 350°F oven for about 25 minutes.

MIDNIGHT SANDWICH (SANDWICH DE MEDIA NOCHE)

Don't be deceived by the name—you can enjoy this sandwich at any time of day! This version of the delightful Cuban sandwich is ideal Super Bowl party fare. I like to make platters of these sandwiches to serve with Yuca Fries (page 76) at afternoon family parties. Accompany with Salpicón de Frutas (page 152) or ice-cold Aguilas (Colombian beer) . MAKES 8 SANDWICHES; SERVES 8

2 tablespoons Dijon mustard

Eight 8-inch-long pieces baguette, halved lengthwise

2 tablespoons mayonnaise

16 thin slices roast pork

16 thin slices smoked ham

8 thin slices white Cheddar cheese

2 large dill pickles, thinly sliced

Salt and pepper to taste

8 teaspoons unsalted butter at room temperature

Heat a sandwich press or preheat the oven to 350°F. Spread mustard on the cut side of the bread tops, and mayonnaise on the cut-side bottoms. On the mayonnaise-coated side of each sandwich, layer 2 pieces each roast pork, ham, and Cheddar cheese. Add some pickle slices. Sprinkle with salt and pepper, then put the top on each sandwich. Butter the outside of each sandwich before placing them in a sandwich press. If you are using the oven, put the sandwiches on a baking pan and place a heavy weight, such as a brick wrapped in aluminum foil or a cast-iron skillet, on top of the sandwiches (try to distribute the weight evenly). Bake until the cheese melts, about 10 minutes. Serve immediately.

LAMB AND GOAT CHEESE EMPANADAS

One of the many benefits I gained from spending a year with highly acclaimed chef Michel Guérard in southern France was learning to combine flavors. My time at Eugenie-les-Bains was filled with new information about ingredients, like goat cheese, niçoise olives, and herbs, that I had not previously cooked with—or even tasted. When I returned to the States, I began to apply my new-found knowledge to my own Latino style of cooking. The results have been *excelentes!* Here, I've fused the classic Latino empanada with the Mediterranean flavors of lamb, goat cheese, and olives. Empanadas, in addition to being quite tasty, are convenient party fare because you can prepare them ahead of time and then heat them up just before your guests arrive. (You can also buy empanada leaves—Goya makes them—and skip the dough-making step.) Serve these tasty pastry pockets with balloon glasses of Mango and Lemongrass Sangría (page 161). MAKES 6

1 teaspoon canola oil, plus oil for deep-frying

8 ounces finely diced or ground lamb

1 green onion, including light green parts, thinly sliced

2 ounces fresh white goat cheese

1 beefsteak tomato, finely diced

6 niçoise olives, pitted and coarsely chopped

1 lime wedge (1/8 of 1 lime)

1 cup precooked cornmeal (*harina precocida*)

1 cup warm water

Kosher salt to taste

In a medium sauté pan or skillet, heat the 1 teaspoon oil over medium heat. Add the lamb and cook until browned. Remove from heat and stir in the green onion, goat cheese, tomato, and olives. Stir to blend. Squeeze the lime wedge over and set aside.

To make the dough: Put the cornmeal in a large bowl. Gradually add the warm water, stirring constantly. Add the salt and mix well with your hands. The dough should feel slightly sticky and elastic. Cover and refrigerate for 10 minutes to set. Line a work surface with a sheet of plastic wrap. Place the dough on top of the plastic and cover with another sheet of plastic. Use a rolling pin to roll the dough to an 1/8-inch thickness. Then, keeping the plastic on top, use a 2 1/2-inch-diameter biscuit or cookie cutter to cut out rounds of dough.

Take off the top layer of plastic wrap and remove the dough between the rounds; set aside. Place 1 heaping teaspoon filling on the bottom half of each circle. Use the plastic wrap to fold each circle over. Seal the edge with your moistened finger. Repeat for each empanada. Reroll the remaining dough and make additional empanadas until you've used up the filling.

In a deep, heavy pot or deep fryer, heat 2 to 3 inches of oil to 365°F. Fry the empanadas, a few at a time, until golden and puffed. Using a skimmer, transfer to a wire rack set on a baking sheet. Serve immediately, or let cool and freeze for up to 3 months. Reheat in a preheated 350°F oven for about 25 minutes, or until heated through.

MANGO AND PEACH GAZPACHO

This refreshing cold soup is an excellent starter for any grilled main dish. Because you have to chill the soup for at least 2 hours, you can make it during the morning of your late-afternoon summer barbecue. SERVES 4

1 ripe mango, peeled, cut from pit, and finely diced

2 cups mango nectar

1 unpeeled peach, pitted and finely diced

1 cup Chardonnay wine

Juice of 1 lime

1 teaspoon rice vinegar

10 fresh mint leaves, stacked, rolled, and cut into fine shreds

Kosher salt to taste

In a large bowl, combine the mango and mango nectar. Add the peach, Chardonnay, lime juice, rice vinegar, and most of the mint leaves. Stir well. Add the salt. Cover and refrigerate for at least 2 hours or up to 5 hours. Garnish with the remaining mint leaves.

TEQUILA-CURED SALMON GRAVLAX

This has to be one of the easiest and most elegant of appetizers. It's also *muy delicioso!*
The salmon is cured in the refrigerator overnight, ready to serve the following day just as your
guests arrive. SERVES 6 TO 8

Four 6-ounce salmon fillets, pin bones and skin removed

Kosher salt to taste

1/2 cup finely shredded mint leaves

3 ripe pears, peeled, cored, and cut into 1/4-inch-thick lengthwise slices

4 tablespoons tequila

Malanga Chips (page 40) and Mango and Lime Relish (Page 30) for serving

Place each fillet on a separate piece of plastic wrap. Lightly salt each fillet. Cover
each fillet with a light blanket of the mint, followed by a layer of pear slices. Sprinkle
1 tablespoon tequila over each fillet and wrap tightly in the plastic wrap so that the
liquid can't escape. Place on a platter and refrigerate overnight.

Just before serving, remove the pear, mint, and salt from each piece of salmon.
Slice the salmon thinly and serve with the chips and relish.

OCTOPUS, SHRIMP, AND YELLOW TOMATO CEVICHE

Part of my crusade for making New Yorkers ceviche lovers is serving tastes of this Peruvian-born dish. During the sweet summer evenings on the terrace at Sonora, many customers request the ceviche taster, which they enjoy with cold glasses of beer after our famously humid Manhattan days. Clean and light in flavor, this particular ceviche is full of color and grace. I've added a bit of *ají amarillo* (spicy yellow chili paste) for spark, but you can control the temperature according to your own taste. This recipe is easily doubled for parties; cook the octopus the night before (in fact, I prefer to do that), and put the ceviche together the morning of your party. Just cover and chill until serving time. SERVES 4

1 cup water

1/4 cup dry white wine

4 large shrimp, shelled and deveined

1 small red onion, finely diced

2 yellow beefsteak tomatoes, cut into 1/4-inch dice

Juice of 4 limes

Juice of 2 oranges

2 pounds blanched octopus (page 176) cut into 1/2-inch dice

2 tablespoons coarsely chopped fresh cilantro

2 teaspoons *ají amarillo* (sold in jars in Latin-American markets), or roasted, seeded, and pureéd serrano chiles

2 tablespoons olive oil

Kosher salt and freshly ground pepper to taste

In a medium saucepan, combine the water and wine. Bring to a boil over medium heat. Add the shrimp and simmer for 3 to 4 minutes, or until it turns pink. Using a slotted spoon, transfer the shrimp to a small bowl with ice to cool.

Meanwhile, in a large bowl, combine the onion, tomatoes, lime and orange juices, and octopus. Stir to blend. Cut the shrimp into $1/4$-inch chunks and add them to the bowl. Add the cilantro, *ají amarillo*, and olive oil. Stir to mix. Add salt and pepper. Cover and refrigerate for at least 2 hours, or up to 12 hours.

ASIAN CEVICHE (CEVICHE CHINO LATINO)

If you love sushi as much as I do, this ceviche is for you! For years we Latinos have been combining the flavors of Asia with those of Latin America. Ginger, soy sauce, and lime flavors combine to make this dish fresh and clean tasting. SERVES 6 TO 8

Juice of 8 limes

1 cup soy sauce

1/4 cup rice vinegar

2 pounds sashimi-grade tuna fillets, skinned and cut into 1/4-inch chunks

3 tablespoons minced (almost to a paste) peeled fresh ginger

4 red bell peppers, seeded, deribbed, and julienned

1 red onion, julienned

6 to 8 thin avocado slices for garnish

In a large ceramic or glass bowl, combine the lime juice, soy sauce, and rice vinegar; stir well. Add the tuna, ginger, bell peppers, and onion. Toss until well blended. Cover and refrigerate for at least 3 hours, or up to 12 hours. Serve in chilled martini glasses. Garnish each with a slice of avocado.

SPICY YELLOWFIN TUNA AND SHRIMP-CHIPOTLE CEVICHE

Mangos and chipotles create a wonderful balance in flavor in this ceviche; perhaps that's why my friend Karen calls it my "yin-yang" ceviche. If you're serving more than 4, estimate about 4 ounces of fish and 2 shrimp per person, and simply multiply the other ingredients or add according to taste. MAKES 4 SERVINGS

8 medium shrimp, shelled and deveined, cut into 1/2-inch pieces

2 chipotle chilies en adobo (found in Latin-American markets), puréed

2 ripe mangos, peeled, cut from pit, and cut into 1/4-inch dice

1/4 cup minced fresh chives

1 cup diced daikon (Japanese white radish)

1/3 cup fresh orange juice

1/2 cup mango juice

1 pound sashimi-grade yellowfin tuna fillets, skinned and cut into 1/2-inch dice

In a large bowl, combine all the ingredients except the tuna. Cover and refrigerate for at least 15 minutes, or up to 3 hours. Add the tuna 10 minutes before serving.

TUNA AND AVOCADO CEVICHE

The grill is going strong. Friends are gathered round, drinking ice-cold beer, and laughing as the sun casts its orange rays at the end of a sultry summer day. This is when I serve cool tuna and avocado ceviche. SERVES 4 TO 6

2 pounds sashimi-grade tuna fillets, skinned and cut into 1/4-inch dice

1/3 cup fresh orange juice

1 cup fresh lime juice

2 ripe Hass avocados, peeled, pitted, and cut into 1/2-inch dice

1/2 cup coarsely chopped fresh cilantro leaves

1/2 cup Pommery or Dijon mustard

1/4 cup extra-virgin olive oil

Kosher salt and freshly ground pepper to taste

Put the tuna in a large glass or ceramic bowl. Add the orange and lime juices, mix well, and cover tightly. Refrigerate for 15 minutes. Add all the remaining ingredients, stir to mix, and refrigerate another 15 minutes, or until the tuna is turning opaque on the outside but is still rare on the inside. Serve chilled.

LOBSTER AND MANGO CEVICHE

The sweet meat of lobster and the tasty flesh of mango blend beautifully with the spark of poblano chilies, radishes, and onions. SERVES 4

6 cups water

4 fresh or thawed frozen lobster tails

$1/4$ cup dry white wine

1 pinch saffron threads

1 cup fresh lime juice

$1^1/_2$ cups mango nectar

4 mangos, peeled, cut from pit, and cut into $1/4$-inch dice

1 poblano chili, roasted and peeled (page 185)

4 small radishes, diced

1 red onion, finely diced

Kosher salt and freshly ground pepper to taste

In a large saucepan, bring the water to a boil. Add the lobster tails, wine, and saffron. Cook for 3 minutes, or until the shells turn bright red. (You want to undercook them, because they will continue to "cook" from the lime juice.) Transfer the tails to a bowl of ice water to cool to the touch.

Remove the lobster meat from the shells and chop into $1/4$-inch chunks. Transfer to a large glass or ceramic bowl. Add the lime juice and mango nectar and mix well. Stir in the mangos, chili, radishes, onion, salt, and pepper. Cover tightly and refrigerate for at least 30 minutes or up to 24 hours. Stir the mixture well before serving.

FILET MIGNON TIRADITO WITH GREEN ONIONS AND OLIVE OIL

This treat is a Peruvian version of Italian carpaccio, sliced raw steak. As with that dish, the key is excellent meat. Tiradito, like carpaccio, must be thinly sliced. SERVES 6

1 1/2 pounds best-quality filet mignon, cut into very thin crosswise slices

1 1/2 cups extra-virgin olive oil

3/4 cup soy sauce

Juice from 2 limes

Juice from 3 oranges

6 green onions, including light green parts, cut into thin lengthwise slices

1/2 cup coarsely chopped fresh cilantro

Refrigerate 6 rimmed dishes for at least 20 minutes. Arrange the filet mignon on the chilled plates. In a bowl, whisk together the olive oil, soy sauce, and lime and orange juices. Add the green onions. Use a pastry brush to brush the sauce over the filet mignon. Sprinkle with cilantro and serve immediately.

CHINO-LATINO TIRADITO

A gorgeous dish that explodes with intense flavor! Serve on a bed of mâche or mixed salad greens.
SERVES 4

1 pound best-quality filet mignon, cut into very thin crosswise slices

2 tablespoons soy sauce

2 teaspoons rice vinegar

4 teaspoons olive oil

2 pinches sugar

2 drops chipotle purée (page 174)

2 tablespoons mango nectar

2 green onions, including green parts, cut into very thin diagonal slices

Finely diced mango and chopped fresh chives for garnish

Freshly ground pepper to taste

Chill a rimmed serving platter in the refrigerator for at least 20 minutes. Arrange the slices of meat on the platter. In a medium bowl, whisk together the soy sauce, vinegar, olive oil, and sugar. Add the chipotle purée, mango nectar, and green onions. Mix well. Use a ladle to evenly distribute the mixture over the meat. Sprinkle the mango, chives, and pepper over. Serve immediately.

DUCK AND SWEET PLANTAIN ROULADE WITH A MANGO GLAZE

My guests quickly succumb to the joys of this *fabuloso* combination. For all you *canard à l'orange* fans, this roulade is a tasty and tropical alternative. The recipe takes time, but it's worth it. Ask your butcher for Long Island Muscovy duck breasts. SERVES 6 TO 8

Mango Glaze:

1 teaspoon unsalted butter

1/2 shallot, minced

1/4 cup dry white wine

2 cups mango nectar

1 teaspoon chipotle purée (page 174)

1 tablespoon Dijon mustard

6 pieces dried mango or papaya, cut into 1/8-inch dice

Kosher salt and freshly ground pepper to taste

3 tablespoons canola oil

3 skinless duck breast halves, about 8 ounces each

Kosher salt to taste

3 ripe plantains, peeled and cut into 1/4-inch dice

1/4 cup finely diced mango

1 cup crushed Malanga Chips (page 40) or Terra Chips (found in large
   supermarkets)

To make the glaze: In a medium saucepan, melt the butter over medium heat and sauté the shallot until softened, 3 to 5 minutes. Add the wine and stir. Pour in the nectar and stir to blend. Stir in the chipotle purée, mustard, and dried mango or papaya. Add the salt and pepper. Simmer over medium heat until reduced by half, about 20 minutes.

Preheat the oven to 350°F. Cover a work surface with 3 sheets of plastic wrap, 1 sheet for each breast. Spread 1 teaspoon canola oil on each piece of plastic wrap. Place a duck breast on each. Sprinkle with salt and cover with another sheet of plastic wrap. Use a mallet or rolling pin to pound the breasts until they're thin enough to be rolled, about 1/4 inch thick.

In a large sauté pan or skillet, heat 1 tablespoon oil over medium heat and sauté the plantains until well browned on both sides. Immediately transfer to a large bowl. Coarsely mash with the back of a wooden spoon (it's important to do this step by hand—a food processor would turn them into a purée). Add the mango and mix well.

Remove the top sheet of plastic wrap and spread the mango mixture evenly over the duck breasts. Using the plastic wrap on the bottom, tightly roll up each breast inside the plastic. Tighten at both ends by making a knot in the plastic wrap.

(continued)

Bring a large pot of water to a boil. Poach each duck breast by placing it in a skimmer and immersing it in the boiling water for just 3 minutes. Remove and let cool to the touch.

Pour the malanga or Terra chips into a jelly-roll pan. In a large ovenproof sauté pan or skillet, heat the remaining 1 tablespoon oil over medium-high heat. Roll the roulades in the chips, then transfer them to the pan and sear them, turning as needed, for 2 to 3 minutes, or until evenly browned. Put the pan in the oven and roast for 3 minutes for medium-rare. Remove from the oven, and cut into 1/4-inch-thick slices. Serve, drizzled with the mango glaze.

CHICKEN BROCHETTES IN A MANGO BARBECUE SAUCE (ANTICUCHOS DE POLLO CON UN MOJO DE MANGO)

These tasty brochettes can be grilled while you and your friends are sipping your Mango Martinis (page 164) around the barbecue. At the restaurant, we use sugarcane skewers because they look great and add a touch of sweetness. To use sugarcane, peel off the tough outer skin, then cut the sugarcane into skewer-sized lengths. Serve these brochettes with Palomino's Sparky Peruvian Potato Salad (page 80). SERVES 6 TO 8

2 cups mango nectar

2 tablespoons ketchup

1 teaspoon chipotle puree (page 174)

1 tablespoon olive oil

1 teaspoon Worcestershire sauce

2 pounds skinless, boneless free-range chicken breasts, cut into strips
1-inch wide, 4-inches long, and 1/2-inch thick

Light a fire in a charcoal or gas grill. Soak 6 to 8 wooden skewers in water for 30 minutes.

In a large, shallow bowl, whisk the mango nectar, ketchup, chipotle purée, oil, and Worcestershire sauce together. Add the chicken and let sit for 15 minutes. Drain the chicken and weave each strip onto a skewer by moving the skewer up and down as if it were a needle. Grill for 3 to 5 minutes on each side, or until opaque throughout. Serve hot or at room temperature.

SIDE DISHES

YUCA FRIES

This is one of the most popular side dishes at Sonora, simply because these fries are *deliciosos!* These can be served at children's birthday parties as a snack, or at grown-up and family parties as an appetizer or side dish. Though many adults and kids enjoy these simply sprinkled with salt (and served with ketchup), I like to serve my yuca fries with a choice of salsas, like Salsa Roja (page 20), guacamole (page 29), or Peruvian Huancaína sauce (page 77). I promise you that once you start making these not only will your guests be asking for more, but you and your family will start craving them. SERVES 8

4 pounds peeled fresh or frozen yuca, cooked (page 186)

Canola oil for deep-frying

Kosher salt for sprinkling

Cut the yuca into $1/2$-inch-thick sticks. Preheat the oven to 250°F and place an oven-proof serving platter inside. In a deep, heavy pot or deep fryer, heat 2 inches of oil to 365°F. Fry a small batch of yuca for 3 to 5 minutes, or until lightly browned. Using a skimmer, transfer to paper towels to drain, then to a large bowl. Sprinkle with salt and toss lightly with your hands. Transfer to the platter in the oven. Repeat to fry the remaining yuca. Serve immediately.

PERUVIAN POTATOES WITH PEPPERED CHEESE SAUCE (PAPAS A LA HUANCAÍNA)

It wasn't until I moved to New York that I had the pleasure of being introduced to a variety of Latin-American cuisines. Of course, I am enamored with my own Colombian cuisine, but I must admit that Peruvian cuisine comes in a close second. Like Colombia, Peru has a wealth of geographic differences, which translate into a plethora of foods. This, combined with influences from the many peoples who have come to the area, has left the country with a treasure chest of dishes. *Papas a la Huancaína,* which originated in the gorgeous snow-capped mountain region of Huancayo and varies slightly from family to family, is a dish that brings a tear to the eye of many Peruvians. This side dish goes beautifully with grilled meats and fish and can be served either warm or cold. You can prepare the salsa and the potatoes ahead of time, then combine them and serve at room temperature. SERVES 8 TO 10

2 pounds small Yukon Gold or new potatoes, scrubbed

Kosher salt to taste

Salsa a la Huancaína:

6 ounces queso blanco (Mexican white cheese) or mold feta cheese

1/2 *ají mirasol,* or 1 teaspoon *ají amarillo* (sold in jars in Latin-American markets, see page 190), 1 guajillo chili, soaked in water until soft and chopped, or 1/4 teaspoon cayenne pepper

One 4-ounce package saltine crackers, crumbled

One 12-ounce can evaporated milk

2 teaspoons ground turmeric

(continued)

    Lettuce leaves for serving

    Peruvian or kalamata olives for garnish

Put the potatoes in a large pot and add water to cover. Add salt and bring the water to a boil. Boil for about 12 minutes, or until the potatoes are cooked through but still firm. Drain and let cool to the touch.

To make the Salsa: Using a blender or food processor, combine the cheese, *ají* or other chili or spice, crackers, milk, and turmeric and process until smooth.

Slice the potatoes 1/4-inch thick. Line a platter with lettuce leaves and place the potatoes on top. Pour the salsa on top (if it's been chilled, stir to soften). Garnish with olives and serve.

SPARKY PERUVIAN POTATO SALAD

My writer for this book, Arlen Gargagliano, was so excited by the combination of flavors—and colors—in this salad that she now serves it at almost every family gathering! She's made it with new potatoes and baby spinach, and with and without the grilled shrimp and corn. In fact, once you've made this salad a few times, you can add and subtract ingredients according to your own *gusto* (taste). SERVES 8 TO 10

6 medium shrimp, shelled and deveined

1 teaspoon garlic oil (page 183)

2 pounds small to medium unpeeled purple, new, or Yukon potatoes

1 tablespoon kosher salt

3 ripe mangos, peeled, cut from pit, and finely diced

6 green onions, including light green parts, thinly sliced

Kernels cut from 4 ears roasted corn, or 2 cups roasted corn kernels (page 184)

1/3 cup Chipotle Mayonnaise (page 174), or to taste

Coarsely chopped fresh chives, for garnish

Rub the shrimp with the garlic oil. Heat a grill pan over medium heat. Cook the shrimp for just 3 minutes on each side, or until pink. Let cool, then cut into 1/4-inch dice.

Put the potatoes in a large, heavy pot and add cold water to cover. Add the salt. Cover, bring to a boil, and cook for about 15 minutes, or until the potatoes can be easily pierced with a knife. Drain and let cool to the touch.

Meanwhile, in a large ceramic or glass bowl, combine the mangos, green onions, grilled shrimp, and corn. Toss to combine.

Cut the potatoes into $1/4$-inch chunks and add them to the bowl. Add the chipotle mayonnaise and toss the contents to coat evenly. Serve immediately, or cover and refrigerate for up to 2 days. Sprinkle with chives prior to serving.

PALOMINO'S RICE WITH BEANS (ARROZ MORO)

Though many people in Colombia make *arroz moro*, the Palomino family variation has been pre-pared in my home for as long as I can remember. This party side dish not only makes a gorgeous presentation, thanks to its colors, it is also very tasty and easy to prepare. (For larger crowds, simply double or triple the recipe.) The beauty of *arroz moro* is that you can make it ahead of time and then heat it up at the last minute. You can also do it in steps: Prepare the rice the previous day and finish it on the day of your party. It keeps for several days in the refrigerator, and it's great for leftovers. Though it goes with just about anything—and my vegetarian friends eat it as a meal—I like to serve it with Roasted Suckling Pig (page 92), Argentine Sirloin Steak (page 108), or Ecuadorian Shrimp with a Chipotle-Citrus Marinade (page 41). SERVES 6

2 1/4 cups chicken stock (page 180) or canned low-salt chicken broth

1 cup long-grain rice, rinsed

1 teaspoon unsalted butter

1 green onion, including light green parts, thinly sliced

1 plum tomato, diced

1 tablespoon fresh or thawed frozen corn kernels

1 clove roasted garlic (page 184)

1 cup cooked black beans (page 175)

1 pinch sazón spice blend (page 187) or ground cumin

Kosher salt and freshly ground pepper to taste

In a medium saucepan, bring 2 cups of stock or broth to a boil. Add the rice, stir, reduce heat to low, cover, and simmer for 15 minutes, or until the rice is al dente (you don't want to cook it completely).

In a large sauté pan or skillet, melt the butter over medium heat and sauté the green onion, tomato, and corn for 5 minutes, or until the corn is tender. Add the garlic and stir to blend. Add the cooked rice and its liquid, the black beans, and the remaining stock or broth. Add the sazón or cumin, salt, and pepper. Cook until heated through, stirring gently. Remove from heat and pour onto a platter. Serve immediately.

4

MAIN DISHES

SEA SCALLOPS WITH A MALANGA CRUST

This is one of those very easy-to-prepare yet dazzling party entrées. The crunchy malanga, which contrasts with the silky smooth sea scallops, is additionally complemented by the Rioja-rich onions. I love this both as an appetizer and as a main *plato* (dish). Serve with Lobster and Mango Ceviche (page 67). SERVES 4 AS A MAIN DISH, 6 TO 8 AS AN APPETIZER

20 Malanga Chips (page 40), or one 6-ounce bag Terra Chips

12 sea scallops

Pinch of kosher salt

2 tablespoons olive oil

Caramelized Onions:

2 tablespoons olive oil

2 red onions, thinly sliced

2 tablespoons sugar

3 cups dry red wine, preferably Rioja

Preheat the oven to 350°F. In a blender or food processor, briefly chop the chips so they're still in visible chunks. Set aside.

Put the scallops in a large bowl and add the salt. Stir. Pour in the chopped chips and mix, using your hands or a wooden spoon, until the scallops are well coated. In a large ovenproof sauté pan or skillet, heat the oil over medium-high heat. Add the

(continued)

scallops and sauté for 2 minutes, or until the chips are brown. Immediately put the pan in the oven and cook the scallops for 5 to 7 minutes, or until they are springy to the touch and opaque throughout.

Meanwhile, make the onions: Heat the oil in a medium saucepan over medium-high heat. Add the onions, sugar, and red wine. Sauté the onions for about 8 minutes, or until deep red and caramelized.

Place the scallops on a warmed large serving dish or individual plates. Using tongs, transfer the onions from the saucepan and to the top of the scallops. Drizzle the wine sauce over. Serve immediately.

CHILEAN SEA BASS A LA CAZUELA

This dish was inspired by renowned California chef Bradley Ogden, with whom I had the privilege of spending some time several years ago. In San Francisco, I discovered a striking resemblance between what was called California cuisine and Colombian cooking! Both use the freshest ingredients to create dishes that are tasty, gorgeous, and healthful. This fish stew is a party natural because it's so easy to prepare. Make your Salsa Criolla ahead of time, and you can put this part of your main course together just before your guests arrive—or even while they're sipping their Passion Fruit Margaritas (page 162). Serve with Palomino's Rice with Beans (page 82) and a green salad.
SERVES 4

Recipe Salsa Criolla (page 24)

Four 8-ounce fillets Chilean or American sea bass

Juice of $1/2$ lemon

Chopped fresh chives and Peruvian or niçoise olives for garnish

Blanket the bottom of a large, $1/2$-inch-deep enameled cast-iron casserole with the salsa criolla. Place the fillets on top in a single layer. Simmer over low heat for 8 to 10 minutes, or until the fish is opaque throughout. Remove from heat and pour the lemon juice over the fillets. Sprinkle with chives, garnish with olives, and serve immediately.

STEAMED MANILA CLAMS IN A CILANTRO-SAFFRON BROTH

This is an ideal dish for small get-togethers in front of a fireplace. Keep plenty of crusty bread handy, because after you eat the clams you'll want to dip into the sauce. I like to serve this family style, with everyone eating from the same dish, along with a bottle of delicious dry white wine.

SERVES 4

3 tablespoons garlic oil (page 183)

36 Manila or littleneck clams, scrubbed

3 1/2 cups chicken stock (page 180) or canned low-salt chicken broth

3 pinches saffron threads

Kosher salt and freshly ground pepper to taste

1 1/2 tablespoons unsalted butter

Juice of 1/2 lemon

1 large beefsteak tomato, seeded and cut into 1/4-inch dice

1 bunch cilantro, stemmed and coarsely chopped

Crusty French or toasted whole-wheat bread

In a large saucepan, heat the garlic oil over medium-high heat. Add the clams and stock or broth. Bring to a boil and cook for 4 to 6 minutes, or until the clams start to open. Add the saffron, salt, and pepper. Cook for 2 minutes. Stir in the butter and lemon juice. Finally, add the tomato and cilantro. Gently stir and simmer for 1 more minute. Remove from heat, pour onto a large platter, and serve immediately, with French or toasted whole-wheat bread.

ROAST SUCKLING PIG (LECHÓN ASADO)

I don't think I've ever had Christmas without the succulent flavors of *lechón!* Talking about roast pig—crispy golden brown on the outside, *jugoso* (juicy) and tender on the inside—will make many a Colombian weak in the knees. Colombia is not alone in its love affair with this fabulous dish; throughout Latin America, and in Spain and Portugal, suckling pig is a favorite. I encourage you to try this new dish for a special occasion. Be sure to plan ahead (the pig should marinate for 12 hours prior to cooking). SERVES 12

1 suckling pig, 12 to 15 pounds

Cloves from 2 heads garlic, coarsely chopped

1/4 cup freshly ground pepper

1 tablespoon kosher salt

1 bottle lager, such as Dos Equis

1 small bunch cilantro, stemmed and coarsely chopped

8 tablespoons canola oil

Have your butcher clean the pig inside and out, remove the eyeballs, and make several cuts on each side of the backbone so the pig doesn't burst during cooking.

In a blender or food processor, combine the garlic, pepper, salt, 1/3 cup of the beer, the cilantro, and 5 tablespoons of the canola oil. Process just until blended. Using your hands, rub half the marinade into the skin of the pig and the other half into the cavity. Put the pig in a large roasting pan, cover loosely with aluminum foil, and refrigerate it for at least 12 hours.

Preheat the oven to 350°F. Prop the pig's mouth open with a piece of foil or wood. Loosely cover the ears and tail with pieces of foil so that they don't burn during cooking. Smear the remaining 3 tablespoons oil over the outside of the pig and place it on a rack in the roasting pan. Put it in the oven and roast for 1 hour.

Remove from the oven and brush with some of the remaining beer. Roast for another 2 1/2 hours, brushing the pig with beer every 30 minutes. Remove the foil from the ears and tail, and increase the oven temperature to 450°F. Roast for 20 to 30 more minutes, or until the skin is a lovely dark brown and very crisp, and the juices run clear when the pig is pricked with a sharp knife.

Carefully remove the pig from the oven. Let cool for about 30 minutes. To carve, cut lengthwise along the backbone and then cut each half crosswise between the ribs into about 6 pieces (you will then have a total of 12 servings).

SWEET AND SOUR LONG ISLAND DUCK BREASTS WITH MASHED PLANTAINS AND POTATOES

Passion fruit, known as *maracuyá* in Spanish, was one of my childhood favorites. Here, I've combined it with another one of my favorites, duck. When I worked with Larry Forgione in An American Place, he taught me different techniques for creating quintessentially tasty duck dishes. The trick of criss-crossing the skin, used here, yields a golden crispy duck. This dish is a great party dish because it's *sabroso* (tasty), but also unique, elegant, and easy to prepare. SERVES 4

Mashed Plantains and Potatoes:

3 very ripe (black) plantains, cut into 1/2-inch chunks

4 Idaho potatoes, peeled and cut into 1/4-inch-thick slices

3 tablespoons unsalted butter

1 tablespoon honey

3 tablespoons heavy cream

3/4 cup walnuts, chopped

4 Long Island duck breast halves, about 12 to 14 ounces each, skin on

1 cup passion fruit nectar or thawed frozen passion fruit pulp, plus sugar to taste if needed

To make the potatoes: In a stockpot, combine the plantains and potatoes. Add water to cover. Bring to a boil and cook for 20 to 30 minutes, or until the potatoes are very

(continued)

soft. Remove from heat and add the butter, honey, cream, and walnuts. Use a potato masher to blend everything together to a chunky consistency. Cover with aluminum foil and set aside.

In a 12-inch skillet over medium heat, sear the duck breasts, skin-side down, for about 10 minutes, or until a rich brown color. (There's so much fat in the skin that you don't need to add any oil to the pan—in fact, you may want to drain some after a bit.) Turn the duck over and add the nectar or pulp so that it covers the surface area of the pan. Cook the duck on the second side until golden brown, about 4 to 6 minutes for medium-rare, turning the breasts over every 2 minutes. Remove from the pan (but don't discard the remaining sauce) and let rest for about 5 minutes, then cut into 1/4-inch-thick slices. Place a bed of the mashed potatoes on each warmed plate, then arrange the slices of duck on top. Drizzle the duck with the pan sauce and serve immediately.

SONORA'S SEARED SALMON WITH CREAMY PEPPER SAUCE (SONORA'S SALMÓN A LA HUANCAÍNA)

If you're entertaining a small group of people whom you would like to dazzle, try serving this simple and fabulously tasty dish. The contrast of the salt-and-peppered seared salmon with the subtle salsa makes for an excellent marriage in terms of flavors, textures, and colors. Serve with Wild Rice (page 126) or Yuca Fries (page 76), and a bottle of dry white wine. SERVES 6

Six 6-to-8-ounce salmon fillets, pin bones and skin removed

Kosher salt and freshly ground pepper to taste

1 tablespoon canola oil

1/4 cup Salsa a la Huancaína (page 77)

Lemon wedges for garnish

Preheat the oven to 350°F. Sprinkle the salmon with salt and pepper. In a large oven-proof sauté pan or skillet, heat the oil over high heat. Sear the salmon for 2 minutes on each side, or until golden brown. Coat the fillets with the Huancaína sauce and bake in the oven for 5 minutes, or until just beginning to flake but still slightly translucent in the center. (Watch your time here; you don't want to overcook the fish.) Serve with lemon wedges.

ROASTED SQUAB WITH BLACK PEPPER AND PANELA

If you're planning a small dinner party and want to make something dazzling and new, try this recipe. Even if you've never cooked squab this is a tasty and gorgeous meal. The freshly ground pepper and *panela*, Colombian brown sugar (or any light brown sugar), sear into the crispy skin and combine to create a delicate balance for the rich squab. The sweet-potato hash browns are a flavorful and beautiful complement to the birds. Start with Peach and Mango Gazpacho (page 57) and serve the squab with Sparky Peruvian Potato Salad (page 80), a mixed green salad, French bread, and a bottle of Rioja wine. SERVES 4 TO 6

4 squab (about 12 ounces each)

Freshly ground pepper to taste

1/2 loaf (8 ounces) *panela* or 1/2 cup packed light brown sugar

1 cup water

3/4 cup chicken stock (page 180) or canned low-salt chicken broth (or as needed)

Sweet-Potato Hash Browns:

3 sweet potatoes, peeled and cut into 1-inch-thick slices

2 teaspoons unsalted butter

1 very ripe (black) plantain, sliced lengthwise and cut into 1/4-inch chunks

3/4 cup chicken stock (page 180) or canned low-salt chicken broth (or as needed)

2 tablespoons thinly sliced green onion

2 tablespoons fresh or thawed frozen corn kernels

2 tablespoons finely diced red beefsteak tomato

Rinse and pat the squab dry. Place the squab on a clean work surface. With a sharp knife or kitchen shears, cut along both sides of each backbone. Remove it and discard. Then cut each bird in half crosswise. On each leg/thigh piece, cut a slit both on the leg and on the thigh so the squab will cook through. Cut off the wing tips. Sprinkle the squab with pepper (the *panela* or brown sugar will soften the blow a bit, but you may want to be conservative the first time you make this). Set aside.

In a large bowl, mix the *panela* or brown sugar and water until the sugar is dissolved. Pour the mixture into a large skillet. Bring to a boil over medium heat. Immediately place the squab, skin-side down, in the skillet (you may have to do this in batches). Sear the skin and caramelize the squab, watching constantly and adding stock or broth as needed to make sure the squab doesn't burn, for 3 to 5 minutes. Turn the squab over and continue to cook, turning the squab every 3 to 5 minutes, and adding stock or broth as needed for about 15 minutes, or until the skin becomes a deep brown color and the meat is medium-rare. Set aside and keep warm.

To make the hash browns:

Cook the sweet potatoes in salted boiling water until al dente, about 10 minutes. Drain, let cool slightly, and cut into 1/4-inch dice.

In a medium saucepan, melt the butter over medium heat. Add the sweet potatoes and plantain. Cook until the sweet potatoes are tender, 5 to 7 minutes, stirring constantly and adding stock or broth as needed if they start to stick. Remove from heat and scrape into a large bowl. Add the green onion, corn, and tomato. Toss to mix. Arrange the sweet-potato mixture on a platter in a bed (you can use a ring mold if you have one) for the squab to rest on. Slice the squab, or keep the pieces as they are and arrange them decoratively on top of the potatoes. Serve immediately.

PALOMINO OXTAIL STEW A LA RIOJA

Whiffs of this stew immediately transport me back to the kitchen of my childhood, where my mother would frequently prepare this *receta familiar* (family recipe) on cool, damp winter days in Bogotá. I can still see her in front of our stove, wearing one of her many half-skirt aprons, lifting a big wooden spoon to her mouth and smiling. Though it takes about 3 hours to prepare this stew, it's well worth the time (and it's great the next day). I often double the recipe, serve half, and freeze half. SERVES 4 TO 6

5 pounds oxtails, trimmed of fat and cut into 2-inch chunks

Kosher salt and freshly ground pepper to taste

1/4 cup canola oil

2 cups Rioja or any dry red wine

2 to 3 quarts chicken stock (page 180) or canned low-salt chicken broth

Leaves from 15 sprigs thyme

1 bay leaf

1 peeled fresh or thawed frozen yuca, cut into 1-inch chunks (see page 186)

1 green plantain, peeled and cut into 1/2-inch cubes

4 to 6 unpeeled new potatoes, cut into 1/4-inch chunks

3 tablespoons minced fresh cilantro

Sprinkle the oxtails with salt and pepper. In a large stockpot, heat the oil over medium heat and brown the oxtails in batches for 3 to 5 minutes, or until browned on all sides. Transfer to a plate.

(continued)

Return all the oxtails to the stockpot. Add the wine and simmer, uncovered, until the wine has almost completely reduced, about 20 minutes. Stir frequently to keep the oxtails from sticking to the bottom.

Add stock or broth to cover, then add the thyme and bay leaf. Bring to a simmer and cook, uncovered, for 2 hours and 15 minutes, adding stock or broth as needed to keep the oxtails covered. Add the yuca, plantain, and potatoes. Cook for another 30 to 45 minutes, or until the vegetables and meat are tender; the meat should be falling off the bone. Serve immediately, sprinkled with cilantro, or let cool, cover, and refrigerate for up to 3 days.

SONORA'S SEAFOOD AND CHORIZO PAELLA

Whenever I'm designing a menu for a large group of people, at the restaurant or at home, paella comes to mind. This one-dish meal, my variation of the classic Spanish version, is great party fare. Paella is one of those dishes that people love but are often intimidated to prepare. Contrary to the rumor that paella takes days to prepare, this dish should take you about 45 minutes. I encourage you to try it. You'll find that it is not difficult, is quite flexible (you can vary the ingredients), and certainly is gorgeous, in addition to being tasty. The way the rice cooks is similar to risotto; you want the rice to constantly drink the liquid, but it must be a gradual process. If you prefer not to quarter the live lobster, you can always substitute more shrimp. Having a 16-inch *paellera*—paella dish— makes the presentation of this meal even more spectacular. SERVES 8

3 small live lobsters, preferably female, about 1¼ pounds each

2 tablespoons olive oil

1 tablespoon minced garlic

24 littleneck clams, scrubbed

7 to 8 cups chicken stock (page 180), fish stock (page 181), or canned low-salt chicken broth

2 pinches saffron threads

1 pinch sazón spice blend (page 187), optional

3 cups long-grain rice, rinsed

Kosher salt and freshly ground pepper to taste

2 fresh Colombian or Mexican chorizos or dried Spanish chorizos, sliced ¼-inch thick on the diagonal

30 large shrimp, shelled and deveined

(continued)

18 mussels, scrubbed and debearded

½ cup *sofrito* (page 26)

Garnish:

1 tablespoon coarsely chopped fresh chives

2 lemons, cut into wedges

Secure the lobster claws with rubber bands. Wrap your hand in a kitchen towel to protect it, and turn the lobster belly-side down. Prepare the lobster by firmly holding the tail down and inserting the tip of a sharp knife into the flesh between the head and the body. (This severs the spinal cord.) Let sit for 2 minutes. Turn the lobster over. Using a sharp chef's knife or kitchen shears, cut the lobster in half from head to tail. Remove the claws and crack them (this facilitates cooking). Discard the intestinal vein behind the tail and the stomach sac behind the head. You will have 4 large pieces of lobster. Repeat with the remaining lobsters.

In a 16-inch paella pan, heat the oil over medium heat. Add the garlic and stir. Add the clams, 5 cups of stock or broth, the saffron, and sazón. Cook until the clams open, 3 to 5 minutes, and transfer the clams to a bowl on the side. Discard any clams that do not open.

Add the rice to the pan, stir, and spread evenly. Add salt and pepper. Place the chorizo on top of the rice and press it in lightly. Add 2 more cups stock or broth and cook for 12 minutes.

Place the lobster pieces on top of the rice. Add more stock or broth if needed (the rice should still be a bit soupy) and cook for 3 minutes. Using a wooden spoon, bury the shrimp in the rice. Add the mussels and cook for another 3 minutes, or until they start to open. (When serving, discard any mussels that have not opened.) Evenly drizzle the *sofrito* on top of the paella and cook for about 2 more minutes, or until all the stock or broth has been absorbed and the rice is tender. Sprinkle with chives, garnish with lemon wedges, and serve immediately.

SKEWERED SHRIMP IN A CAIPIRINHA MARINADE

At Sonora, we skewer our shrimp on sugarcane, but wooden skewers are an easy substitute. The caipirinha—Brazil's national cocktail—brings out the best in shrimp. Customers love this dish all year-round, but claim that it brings in the tropical sun on a wintry day. SERVES 6

Caipirinha Glaze:

1 recipe Caipirinha (page 153)

1 cup mango nectar

1 cup pineapple juice

2 recipes Caipirinha (page 153)

1 tablespoon minced garlic

1 tablespoon olive oil

24 medium shrimp, shelled and deveined

Soak 6 wooden skewers in water for 30 minutes. Prepare a fire in an outdoor grill. You can also use a grill pan heated over high heat.

To make the glaze: In a medium saucepan, combine all the glaze ingredients. Bring to a rapid simmer and cook to reduce by half.

In a medium bowl, mix the caipirinha, garlic, and olive oil together. Place the shrimp in a large, shallow dish. Pour the caipirinha mixture on top and marinate at room temperature for about 5 minutes.

Drain the skewers. Oil the grill grids or grill pan, if using. Thread the shrimp on the skewers and grill until pink, about 3 minutes on each side. Serve hot or at room temperature, with the glaze alongside for dipping.

ARGENTINE SIRLOIN STEAK TOPPED WITH SONORA MOLE

Here, I've combined my version of a Mexican mole sauce with a succulent piece of Argentine steak. If you can't get Argentine steak, any good-quality sirloin will do. I like to serve this dish with ice-cold Dos Equis beer and Sparky Peruvian Potato Salad (page 80). SERVES 6

Mole:

2 cups (8 ounces) slivered almonds

7 poblano chilies, seeded and coarsely chopped

2 cups water

1 green plantain, peeled and coarsely chopped

3 plum tomatoes, coarsely chopped

1/2 cup coarsely chopped fresh cilantro

1/2 cup raisins

3 ounces semi-sweet chocolate, chopped

One 8-inch flour tortilla or small bread roll, torn into small pieces

Six 12-ounce sirloin steaks, trimmed

1 teaspoon olive oil

Kosher salt and freshly ground pepper to taste

To make the mole: preheat the oven to 400°F. Spread the almonds out in a jelly-roll pan and toast them in the oven for about 8 minutes, or until lightly browned (keep an eye on them; you don't want them to burn). Immediately pour them into a bowl.

In a medium saucepan, combine the poblanos and water. Bring to a simmer and cook for about 10 minutes. Add the plantain, tomatoes, cilantro, raisins, chocolate, and tortilla or roll. Continue simmering for about 15 minutes, or until well blended. Add the toasted almonds. In a blender or food processor, blend the mole until smooth.

Prepare an outdoor grill or heat a grill pan over high heat. Rub the steaks with oil and sprinkle both sides with salt and pepper. Grill the steak for 8 to 10 minutes for medium-rare, turning as needed. Serve the steak with a dollop of the mole on top. Serve the remaining mole alongside so that guests can help themselves to more.

CHIMICHURRI LAMB CHOPS WITH GOAT CHEESE

This dish is a *gran mezcla*, or mixture, of my Latin-American heritage and French culinary education. Not only does the marriage of flavors work well (seared lamb with cilantro pesto, complemented by smooth goat cheese), the preparation and cooking times for this dish are minimal. Have your butcher French the rib bones; scraping off the meat makes for an elegant presentation, easy to serve and eat. For a larger party, double the amounts. SERVES 4

2 1/2 cups loosely packed fresh cilantro leaves (about 2 bunches, stemmed), plus a few sprigs for garnish

2/3 cup olive oil

4 cloves garlic, peeled

8 oil-packed sun-dried tomatoes, drained, or 4 teaspoons sun-dried tomato pesto

Kosher salt and freshly ground pepper to taste

16 lamb chops, Frenched

6 ounces fresh white goat cheese at room temperature

In a blender or food processor, combine the cilantro, olive oil, garlic, and sun-dried tomatoes or tomato pesto. Process until smooth. Pour into a shallow dish.

Salt and pepper both sides of the lamb chops and place them on a large platter. Grasp each chop by the bone and dip the meaty part into the cilantro mixture. Be sure to coat the meat on both sides. Return them to the platter.

(continued)

Heat a medium-size sauté pan or skillet over medium-high heat (you don't need to add oil). Working in batches, sear the lamb chops by cooking them for 2 minutes on each side. Turn and sear again on each side for 2 minutes. While searing the last side, use a tablespoon to spread a dollop of goat cheese over the meaty area of the chop. *¡Cuidado!* Careful! The chops and pan will be quite hot. You may need to use a pot holder to grasp the chop with one hand as you spread the goat cheese with the other. These chops should be medium-rare (springy to the touch). Remove from the pan and arrange on a large platter. Garnish with cilantro sprigs and serve.

SWEET AND SOUR SQUAB WITH PLANTAIN POLENTA

Just as in a good marriage—or any good relationship—one of the best qualities of Colombian cooking is its balance. This dish matches the hearty flavor of the squab with the mild taste of polenta.
Cooking the squab in a chipotle-kissed sauce adds a bit of spark, which is softened by the honey and
mango juice. The presentation of this dish is gorgeous: The golden squab rests on a cushion of
sweet-plantain polenta, with a final *toque* (touch) of cinnamon on top. *¡Qué belleza!* How beautiful!

SERVES 4 TO 6

Marinade:

Kosher salt and freshly ground pepper to taste

1/2 cup canola oil

3 tablespoons chipotle purée (page 174)

2 tablespoons dry white wine

1 tablespoon honey

1 tablespoon Pommery or Dijon mustard

1 cup mango nectar

4 squab (about 12 ounces each)

2 tablespoons canola oil

Polenta:

2 very ripe black plantains

1/3 cup water

1/3 cup precooked cornmeal *(harina precocida)*

(continued)

2 tablespoons honey

4 tablespoons unsalted butter at room temperature

1/2 cup chicken stock (page 180) or canned low-salt chicken broth

Dash of ground cinnamon

To make the marinade: In a large bowl, whisk together all the marinade ingredients. Roll each squab in the marinade to coat on all sides. Set the squab aside and reserve the marinade.

Preheat the oven to 400°F. In a medium skillet, heat the 2 tablespoons oil over medium heat. Using tongs, pick up one squab at a time and sear it, turning as necessary, until browned on all sides. Put all the squab in a roasting pan and roast for 12 minutes for medium-rare. Remove them from the oven and let rest for 10 minutes.

To make the polenta: In a large bowl, combine the plantains, water, and cornmeal. Mash the plantains with a fork or the back of a wooden spoon to make a chunky purée. Mash in the honey and butter and set aside.

In a medium skillet, combine the plantain mixture and stock or broth. Cook over medium heat for 3 to 4 minutes, or until heated through, while mashing to the consistency of mashed potatoes. Spread the mixture on a warm platter. Meanwhile, in a small saucepan, boil the reserved marinade for 5 minutes.

Using a sharp knife or poultry shears, cut each squab along both sides of the backbone. Remove the backbone and discard. Cut each bird in half crosswise. Cut the wings off and discard them. Arrange the squab pieces on the polenta, pour the marinade over, and sprinkle very lightly with cinnamon. Serve immediately.

CLASSIC ANDEAN STEW (CHUPE ANDINO)

A steamy *chupe* is always welcome on brisk days; it fills the air with luscious smells and will fill you and your guests with delight. This simple *chupe* should be served with a delicious bottle of wine, crusty French bread, and a green leafy salad. SERVES 4

2 tablespoons olive oil

3 teaspoons minced garlic

2 red beefsteak tomatoes, cut into 1/4-inch dice

2 yellow beefsteak tomatoes, cut into 1/4-inch dice

4 cups chicken stock (page 180) or canned low-salt chicken broth

6 littleneck clams, scrubbed

Pinch saffron threads

12 mussels, scrubbed and debearded

2 teaspoons coarsely chopped fresh cilantro

Kosher salt and freshly ground black pepper to taste

8 medium shrimp, shelled and deveined

4 ounces red snapper fillet, cut into 4 chunks

4 green onions, including green parts, thinly sliced

1/2 lime, cut into wedges

Chopped fresh chives for garnish

In a stockpot, heat the oil over medium heat and sauté the garlic until softened, about 3 minutes. Stir in the tomatoes and stock or broth. Bring to a simmer and add the clams and saffron. Cover and cook for about 5 minutes, or until the clams have opened. Add the mussels, cilantro, salt, pepper, shrimp, red snapper, and the green onions. Cover and simmer until the shrimp are pink and the snapper is opaque throughout, 3 to 5 minutes. Discard any clams or mussels that do not open. Spoon into soup bowls, squeeze a section of lime over each serving, and sprinkle with chives. Serve immediately.

SEARED LONG ISLAND DUCK BREASTS WITH A GUAVA AND AGUARDIENTE CHUTNEY

When I lived in France, I grew to admire how the French incorporated Pernod into their cooking. I realized that I could do the same with my own native country's liquor. This fabulous duck dish boasts an exotic combination of flavors, guaranteed to woo your guests. Serve with Mashed Plantains and Potatoes (page 94). SERVES 6

Six 12-ounce Long Island duck breast halves, skin on

Guava and Aguardiente Chutney:

5 ounces aguardiente (Colombian brandy) or Greek ouzo

$1^1/_2$ cups guava purée

1 teaspoon ground cloves

$^1/_8$ teaspoon ground cinnamon

2 small onions, halved

10 fresh mint leaves

2 tablespoons rice vinegar

3 teaspoons sugar

In a large sauté pan or skillet over low to medium heat, sear each of the duck breasts, skin-side down, for 8 to 10 minutes, or until crispy. (No oil is necessary.)

Meanwhile, make the chutney: In a blender, combine all the chutney ingredients and purée until smooth. Set aside.

Heat a grill pan over medium heat and cook the duck breasts on each side for a total of 3 to 5 minutes, or until medium-rare. Place on warmed serving plates and top with the chutney.

SEARED CHILEAN SALMON IN A CAIPIRINHA GLAZE

The colors of this caramelized salmon, reminiscent of seaside sunsets, will inspire you. The outside is slightly toasted; the inside melts in your mouth. Caipirinha is a perfect partner for Chilean salmon. This is one of those dishes that you can easily prepare while talking with friends in your kitchen. But stand back from the stove: The flames can jump into the pan as the caipirinha dances around the salmon fillet. This dish is simply *maravilloso!* MAKES 4 SERVINGS

1 tablespoon canola oil

Four 6-ounce Chilean or American salmon fillets, pin bones and skin removed

4 recipes Caipirinha (page 153), strained, or 1 cup white rum

Arugula or mixed salad greens for garnish

In a large sauté pan or skillet, heat the oil over high heat and sear the salmon on one side for 4 to 6 minutes, or until browned. Turn the salmon and pour the caipirinha or rum around it. Cook over high heat for 8 to 10 minutes (depending on the thickness of the salmon), or until the fillets are browned on the second side and just slightly translucent in the center. Serve on a bed of arugula or mixed greens.

PERUVIAN LAYERED CASSEROLE (CAUSA)

This is my variation of the classic Peruvian *causa*, a layered potato casserole. Though I usually serve this for dinner, with a bottle of wine, crusty French bread, and a green salad, it can also be served as an appetizer in individual ramekins. SERVES 6

12 small new potatoes (about 4 pounds)

Pinch of kosher salt

2 tablespoons olive oil

1/2 teaspoon Pommery or Dijon mustard

Two 1/2-inch-thick 8-ounce sashimi-grade tuna steaks, cut in half crosswise

One 6-ounce jar marinated artichoke hearts, marinade reserved

10 Peruvian or kalamata olives, pitted

1/2 clove roasted garlic (page 184)

4 tablespoons unsalted butter

Put the potatoes in a large, heavy stockpot, add water to cover, and bring to a boil. Add salt and cook for about 20 minutes, or until very soft.

Meanwhile, heat 2 tablespoons of the oil in a heavy sauté pan or skillet over medium-high heat. Rub the tuna with mustard and sear for 4 to 6 minutes on each side for medium-rare. Remove from the pan and set aside. Add the artichoke hearts and their marinade and the olives to the pan and cook for 2 minutes. Set aside.

(continued)

Drain the potatoes and transfer them to a large bowl. Add the garlic and butter. Using a potato masher or electric mixer, mash until smooth (the only chunks should be the skin).

Spread half of the potatoes in the bottom of an 8-inch square baking dish. Place the tuna on top of the potatoes without overlapping the steaks. Place the artichokes and olives on top. Spread the remaining potatoes on top. Serve immediately or at room temperature.

MANGO-CHIPOTLE GRILLED QUAIL

Quail—known in Bogotá as *codorniz*—is popular Colombian fare. I like them because they're tasty, easy to work with, and very well received. This dish combines beautifully with Sparky Peruvian Potato Salad (page 80). You can save time by making the sauce the day before. At home I like to grill while my guests are sipping their cool Passion Fruit Margaritas (page 162) and munching on Malanga Chips and Yuca Chips (page 40). SERVES 4

8 partially boned quail, butterflied

1 cup mango nectar

1 tablespoon coarsely chopped fresh cilantro

3 tablespoons chipotle purée (page 174)

1/4 cup minced red onion

Dash of ground cumin

Kosher salt and freshly ground pepper to taste

Mixed salad greens for serving

Prepare an outdoor grill, or use a grill pan. Fold the wings on each quail under on the back. Set the quail aside.

In a large baking dish, whisk together all the remaining ingredients except salad greens. Put the quail in the dish and turn to coat both sides.

Oil the grill grids, if using a grill. If using a grill pan, heat it over high heat and brush it with oil. Lift the quail from the marinade and grill for about 3 minutes on each side, or until the juices run clear when the thighs are pierced with a knife. Serve on a bed of mixed salad greens.

PERUVIAN PEPPER CHICKEN (AJÍ DE GALLINA)

Home cooking and comfort foods vary from country to country, and even from city to city. If you were to survey a large number of Peruvians, however, you'd find this to be among their favorite comfort foods. *Ají de gallina*, shredded chicken in a creamy pepper sauce, is not difficult to make, and it's one of those dishes that both adults and children find *muy sabroso*, or very tasty. You can make this a couple of days ahead, reheat it slowly (with a bit of water and/or milk over a low flame), and serve it, Peruvian style, on a bed of rice. *Ají de gallina* recipes vary from zone to zone, but this one was inspired by my friends, sisters Marita and Leda Agurto, who hail from Chiclayo, Peru. You can turn the temperature up or down, depending on the amount of *ají* you use. SERVES 6

4 large boneless, skinless free-range chicken breast halves

1 *ají mirasol*, or 1 teaspoon *ají amarillo*, or 1 guajillo chili, soaked to soften, or ¼ teaspoon cayenne pepper

One 12-ounce can evaporated milk

One 4-ounce package saltines, crumbled into small pieces

6 ounces queso blanco (Mexican white cheese) or mild feta cheese, cut into square chunks

1 teaspoon canola oil

½ red onion, finely diced

½ teaspoon ground turmeric

Steamed rice for serving

Peruvian or kalamata olives for garnish

In a large saucepan of barely simmering salted water to cover, poach the chicken breasts for about 20 minutes, or until opaque throughout. Remove the chicken from the water and let cool to the touch, reserving the broth. Using your hands, shred the chicken into thin 1-inch-long pieces. Set aside.

In a blender or food processor, combine the *ají* or other seasoning, evaporated milk, saltines, and cheese. Mix until puréed. Set aside.

In a medium saucepan, heat the oil over medium heat. Sauté the onion and turmeric until the onions are soft, about 3 minutes. Add the milk mixture and stir. Reduce heat to low. Stir in the chicken, followed by about 2 cups of the reserved broth from cooking the chicken, and cook for 8 to 10 minutes, or until the mixture starts to thicken. Turn off heat. Taste and adjust the seasoning. Serve with rice, garnished with olives.

YUCA-CRUSTED YELLOWFIN TUNA STEAKS ON A BED OF WILD RICE

My Sonora customers are *locos* for my yuca-crusted tuna. Probably they, like me, got tired of the thick, tasteless breadings that mask the flavor of so many fine pieces of fish. The mango-sparked wild rice adds a very special touch in terms of both flavor and color. This rice can be served warm or at room temperature (it's great as a summertime salad). SERVES 6

Wild Rice:

2³/₄ cups water

1 cup wild rice

1 teaspoon unsalted butter

4 ounces dried mango, cut into thin 2-inch-long strips

¹/₄ cup raisins

3 green onions, including green parts, thinly sliced

1 cup fresh or thawed frozen corn kernels

¹/₂ cup mango nectar

Pinch of cumin

¹/₂ red onion, thinly sliced, blanched for 2 minutes, and drained

2 tablespoons Peruvian Thyme-Niçoise Sauce (page 25)

Six ³/₄-inch-thick 8-ounce sashimi-grade yellowfin tuna steaks

Kosher salt and freshly ground pepper to taste

4 cups Yuca Chips (page 40), or 1 bag Terra Chips

2 tablespoons canola oil

Lemon wedges for garnish

(continued)

To make the rice: in a medium saucepan, bring the water to a boil. Add the rice and stir. Reduce heat to low, cover, and simmer for 45 minutes, or until tender. Remove from heat and let sit, covered, for 5 minutes. In a medium sauté pan or skillet, melt the butter over medium heat. Add the mango, raisins, and green onions and stir. Add the rice, corn, and mango nectar and mix. Add the cumin, red onion, and sauce. Stir to mix well. Remove from heat and set aside.

Preheat the oven to 400°F. Sprinkle the tuna with salt and pepper. In a food processor, pulse the chips to crumbs (take care not to grind them too fine). Pour them into a shallow bowl.

Coat each steak on each side by dredging it in the crumbs. In a large skillet, heat the oil over medium heat. Using tongs, put the steaks in the hot oil and sear on each side for about 2 minutes, being careful not to let the crumbs burn (they should be browned). Transfer to a baking pan large enough to hold all the fillets. Transfer to the oven and bake for 1 minute for medium-rare. Make a bed of wild rice on each warmed plate and place the fillets on top. Garnish with lemon wedges and serve.

ARGENTINE HAMBURGERS

Everyone—or almost everyone—loves a great burger! Whether we're grilling outside in the summer, inside during football season, or at the restaurant, this burger is a big hit. I generally prepare the meat ahead of time and cook it to order. For those who like cheese on top, simply add a few slices of Monterey Jack. This recipe can be easily multiplied. Serve with Sparky Peruvian Potato Salad (page 80) or a green salad. SERVES 4

2 pounds ground sirloin beef

3 tablespoons garlic oil (page 183)

$1/4$ cup Argentine Pesto (page 21)

4 sesame sandwich rolls, split in half

Sliced avocado and cheese, and/or lettuce leaves, for serving

In a large bowl, combine the beef, garlic oil, and pesto. Using your hands, mix well to blend. Divide the meat into four $1/2$-inch-thick patties. Let rest for about 15 minutes. (You can also refrigerate the meat at this point to be grilled later. Remove it from the refrigerator 30 minutes before cooking.)

Heat a grill pan over high heat for 2 minutes. Oil the pan and cook the burgers for 5 minutes on each side for medium-rare. Serve on buns, with slices of avocado, cheese, and/or leafy green lettuce.

TUNA AND CHIPOTLE BURGERS

Are you tired of serving the same type of Super Bowl party fare? This burger adds spice to the traditional U.S. festival of football. My patrons—and family members—always request this, even when it's not Super Bowl season! SERVES 4

1 cup plain yogurt

1 tablespoon chipotle purée (page 174)

2 pounds sashimi-grade tuna fillets, cut into $1/4$-inch dice

1 cup Malanga Chips (page 40), or Terra Chips, crushed, plus more chips for serving

5 green onions, including light green parts, finely diced

2 tablespoons Pommery or Dijon mustard

1 cup dried bread crumbs

Kosher salt to taste

4 soft rolls

In a medium bowl, combine the yogurt and chipotle purée. Stir with a fork until well blended. In a large bowl, use your hands or a wooden spoon to mix the tuna, malanga chip crumbs, and yogurt mixture together. Add the green onions, mustard, bread crumbs, and salt. Mix to blend. Cover and refrigerate for about 20 minutes to bind the mixture. Form into four $1/2$-inch-thick patties.

Heat a grill pan over medium heat for 2 minutes. Oil the pan and cook the burgers for 3 to 5 minutes on each side for medium-rare. Serve on soft rolls, with malanga chips.

DESSERTS

FRIED SPANISH DOUGHNUTS WITH DULCE DE LECHE SAUCE (CHURROS DELGADOS CON SALSA DE DULCE DE LECHE)

Don't be scared off by the word *fried*. These tasty treats are *fabulosos!* When I visited Spain several years ago, we topped off an evening of tapas eating and wine drinking with a late night visit to the local *churrería*, where we enjoyed freshly fried churros and thick hot chocolate. (When I commented to a Spanish friend that *churros* were wonderful, she said, "That's why we call our handsome men *churros!*") Recently, I was helping a friend with a party and she didn't have the usual *churro*-making pastry bag, but one that's used for decorating cakes and has a much smaller opening. The little *churros* were easier to make and less oily than the usual thick ones, and they became the basis for this dessert. Either way, I know you and your guests will agree that these *churros* are *riquísmos*, or very delicious! SERVES 4 TO 6

2 cups water

3 tablespoons unsalted butter at room temperature

2 1/2 cups all-purpose flour, sifted

2 large eggs at room temperature

3 tablespoons plus 3/4 cup sugar

Pinch of kosher salt

Canola oil for deep-frying

Sauce:

1 3/4 cups heavy cream

Dulce de Leche (page 178)

In a medium saucepan, heat the water over medium-high heat and add the butter, stirring. Add the flour and stir until smooth with a strong whisk (the mixture will quickly thicken). Reduce heat to low. Whisk in the eggs one at a time, then the 3 tablespoons of sugar and the salt. Remove from heat and let rest for 2 minutes.

Spread the 3/4 cup sugar onto a pie plate (the sugar should be about 1/8 inch deep). Line another plate with paper towels.

In a deep, heavy pot or deep fryer, heat 3 inches oil to 365°F. Scrape the batter into a pastry bag fitted with a fluted nozzle 1/4 inch in diameter. Working in batches, squeeze 3-inch-long pieces of batter into the hot oil and cook the *churros* until browned, 3 to 4 minutes. Using a skimmer, transfer to the paper towels to drain briefly, then roll in sugar to coat.

Quickly make the sauce: In a medium saucepan, bring the heavy cream just to a simmer over low heat. Add the dulce de leche and whisk until blended. Remove from heat. Immediately drizzle on the *churros*, using a spoon or a squeeze bottle, and serve.

ARLEN'S TOASTED-PECAN BROWNIES

When my writer for this cookbook, Arlen, lived in Peru for a year, she introduced the wonders of her brownies to the South American continent. Since then, she's made them for the people of the Dominican Republic, Costa Rica, Colombia, Brazil, Argentina, Chile, and Mexico and they've all loved them! Though she makes many different kinds of brownies (fudge, with nuts, mocha), she says that the secret to great brownies is excellent chocolate and high-quality vanilla (both of which are easily found throughout Latin America). Though Arlen swears by Peruvian chocolate and Dominican vanilla, domestic brands also work quite well. Toasting the pecans prior to baking enhances their flavor (of course, you can always skip them for a non-nut crowd). MAKES SIXTEEN 2-INCH BROWNIES

1/2 cup pecans

2 ounces unsweetened chocolate, chopped

1/2 cup (1 stick) unsalted butter, cut into chunks

2 eggs

1 cup sugar

2 teaspoons vanilla extract

3/4 cup all-purpose unbleached flour

1/2 cup semisweet chocolate morsels

Preheat the oven to 350°F. Butter an 8-inch square baking pan. Spread the pecans in a jelly-roll pan and toast in the oven for 5 to 8 minutes, or until fragrant. Pour the nuts into a bowl, leaving the oven on.

In a medium saucepan, melt the chocolate with the butter over very low heat. Stir until smooth and remove from heat. Stir in the eggs, sugar, and vanilla just to combine. Add the flour and nuts and mix just to blend. Scrape into the prepared pan and spread evenly. Scatter the chocolate morsels evenly over the top.

Bake for about 30 minutes, or until a toothpick inserted in the center comes out almost clean. Let cool for 20 to 30 minutes, then cut into squares. Serve plain or with ice cream on top.

DARK RUM AND PINEAPPLE UPSIDE-DOWN CAKE

Caramelizing the pineapple in rum adds a flavor that sends me right to the tropics! I like to serve this cake at Sunday afternoon get-togethers. SERVES 8

1 pineapple, peeled, quartered, and cored

2 teaspoons vanilla extract

2 tablespoons Myers's rum

1/2 cup plus 6 tablespoons (1 3/4 sticks) unsalted butter at room temperature

3/4 cup sugar

4 eggs, beaten

3/4 teaspoon baking powder

1 1/2 cups unbleached all-purpose flour

Preheat the oven to 350°F. Lightly butter a 9-inch glass pie plate.

Cut the pineapple quarters into 1/2-inch-thick triangles. Put the pineapple in a medium shallow bowl or baking dish. In a small bowl, whisk the vanilla and rum together. Pour the vanilla and rum over the pineapple. Let sit for about 5 minutes.

Heat a large skillet over medium-high heat. Using the tongs, transfer the pineapple to the pan in batches and sauté, using the tongs to turn the pineapple constantly, until browned on each side, 5 to 10 minutes.

(continued)

Cover the bottom of the dish with 1 layer of the pineapple. Dice the remaining larger pieces and fit them in between the spaces wherever possible. Pour the liquid over.

In a medium bowl, cream the butter and sugar together until light and fluffy. Add the eggs and beat until smooth. In a medium bowl, stir the baking powder and flour together well. Add to the wet ingredients and stir until smooth. Scrape the batter over the pineapple and smooth with a spatula. Bake for 30 to 40 minutes, or until a knife inserted in the center of the cake comes out clean. Remove from the oven and set on a wire rack. Let rest for 15 minutes, then unmold onto a plate. Serve now, or cover and refrigerate for up to 3 days.

COLOMBIAN DULCE DE LECHE RICE PUDDING

Just mentioning this *postre* (dessert) to native Colombians will make them moist-eyed with nostalgia. Colombian comfort food is worth the constant attention required. Our *tres leches*, or three-milk, rice pudding is traditionally served during Christmastime, but you can serve it any time. I know a lot of people who enjoy this treat both as an after-dinner dessert and an early-morning breakfast.

SERVES 6

1 cup long-grain white rice

4 cups milk

One 12-ounce can evaporated milk

One 14-ounce can sweetened condensed milk

3/4 cup raisins

In a medium saucepan, combine the rice and 4 cups milk. Bring to a simmer, stirring constantly, and cook to reduce by half. Add the evaporated and sweetened condensed milks. Cook, stirring constantly to prevent scorching, for about 30 minutes or until the mixture starts to thicken. Stir in the raisins.

Pour into a 9-by-13-inch pan and smooth with a spatula. Cover with a paper towel to prevent a skin from forming and let rest for 30 minutes. Remove the paper towel and serve now, or cover with plastic wrap and refrigerate for up to 1 week. Spoon into ramekins or plates to serve.

PERUVIAN DOUGHNUTS (PICARONES)

When I first visited Peru several years ago, I fell in love with *picarones*. These tasty doughnuts, made with a dough of *camote*, or sweet potato, and *zapallo*, or pumpkin, served steaming hot and bathed in a cinnamon-and-orange-scented *miel*, or syrup, are a delightful finish to any meal (or a great start to any day)! Peruvians typically eat their *picarones* by dipping them into the syrup in order to soak it up. Though it's not the Peruvian style, I like to add a couple of scoops of vanilla ice cream, topped with a blanket of *miel*, to delicately melt over my *picarones*. SERVES 8 TO 10

Dough:

One 16-ounce sweet potato, peeled and cut into chunks

1-pound sugar pie pumpkin or acorn squash, seeded, peeled, and cut into chunks

6 cups water

1 cinnamon stick

3 cloves

1 package active dried yeast

1/2 cup warm (105° to 115°F) water

1 teaspoon sugar

2 eggs

3 cups unbleached all-purpose flour

Canola oil for deep-frying

Syrup:

2 cups water

2 cups firmly packed light brown sugar

2 prunes

6 cloves

1 cinnamon stick

Stripped zest of ¹/₂ orange

In a medium saucepan, combine the sweet potato, pumpkin or squash, 6 cups water, cinnamon stick, and cloves. Bring to a boil, reduce heat to a simmer, and cook for about 50 minutes, or until quite soft. Remove from heat (but do not drain) and remove the cloves and cinnamon stick. Using a potato masher, mash the vegetables in the water until they become the consistency of mashed potatoes. Push the mixture through a fine-mesh sieve with the back of a large spoon, or purée it in a blender or food processor. Transfer to the bowl of a heavy-duty mixer.

In a small bowl, combine the yeast, warm water, and sugar. Stir well and set aside until foamy, about 10 minutes. Beat the eggs into the sweet-potato mixture. Beat in the flour ¹/₂ cup at a time until well mixed. Add the yeast mixture and use the bread hook to beat the dough for about 5 minutes, or until well blended. Place a clean dish towel over the bowl and let the dough rise in a warm place for about 45 minutes, or until doubled in size.

Meanwhile, to make the syrup: In a medium saucepan, bring the 2 cups water to a simmer over medium heat. Add the brown sugar and stir until it dissolves. Add the prunes, cloves, cinnamon stick, and orange zest. Simmer, stirring frequently, until thickened, about 20 minutes. Using a slotted spoon, remove the prunes, cloves, and cinnamon stick. Keep the syrup warm over hot water.

(continued)

Fill a bowl with water, add a pinch of salt, and set the bowl next to the bowl of dough. In a deep, heavy pot or deep fryer, heat 2 inches oil to 365°F. Dip your hands into the bowl of water (this will make the dough easier to handle) and pick up about $1/4$ cup of the dough in your hands. Form the dough into a doughnut shape and drop it into the hot oil. Repeat, making 3 or 4 *picarones*, and cook them on one side until browned, about 5 minutes. Use chopsticks or tongs to gently turn the *picarones* over and cook until browned on the second side, about 3 minutes. Using a skimmer, transfer to paper towels to drain. Repeat to fry all the dough. Serve hot, with the syrup poured over.

DULCE DE LECHE FLOURLESS CHOCOLATE CAKE

Chocolate-lovers swoon over this one! I like to balance this rich chocolate cake with a dollop or two of excellent vanilla ice cream—but I'll leave that up to you. I recommend making this cake the morning of your party, then serving it at room temperature with glasses of cold milk or cups of hot Colombian coffee. SERVES 8

- 1 pound semisweet chocolate, chopped
- 6 eggs, separated
- 2 tablespoons Dulce de Leche (page 178)
- Vanilla ice cream for serving (optional)

Preheat the oven to 350°F. Butter a 9-inch springform pan.

In a double boiler, melt the chocolate over barely simmering water. Remove from heat, pour into a large bowl, and set aside.

In a large bowl, beat the egg whites until soft peaks form. In a medium bowl, beat the egg yolks until well blended. Fold the yolks into the melted chocolate, then fold in the whites. Pour the chocolate mixture into the prepared pan. Spoon the dulce de leche into the center of the chocolate mixture. Smooth the top with a spatula.

Place in the oven and bake for 40 minutes, or until a toothpick inserted in the center comes out almost clean. Remove from the oven and let cool in the pan on a wire rack for 30 minutes. Place on a serving plate and remove the sides of the pan. Serve warm or at room temperature, with vanilla ice cream, if you like.

SOFIA'S DULCE DE LECHE OATMEAL COOKIES

Arlen Gargagliano is not only my friend and coauthor, she's also someone who has loved making cookies for as long as she can remember. After falling in love with the creamy flavor of dulce de leche, she came up with these wonderfully crispy lace cookies, which are named after one of her greatest cookie fans: her daughter, Sofia. MAKES ABOUT 6 DOZEN COOKIES

1 cup quick-cooking oats

1 cup sugar

1/2 teaspoon salt

3 tablespoons flour

1 egg, slightly beaten

1/2 cup (1 stick) unsalted butter, melted

1 1/2 teaspoons vanilla extract

2 tablespoons Dulce de Leche (page 178)

Preheat the oven to 350° F. In a large bowl, stir the oats, sugar, salt, and flour together well. Stir in the egg, butter, vanilla, and dulce de leche until well blended. Cover and refrigerate for at least 1 hour, or up to 3 days.

Line 2 baking sheets with aluminum foil, shiny-side up. Scoop up 3/4 teaspoonfuls of dough and place them 2 inches apart on the prepared pans.

Bake for 8 to 10 minutes, or until lightly browned. Remove from the oven and let cool on the pans. Peel off the foil. Repeat for the remaining dough. Serve now, or store in an airtight container for up to 5 days. You can also freeze the cookies, layered on wax paper, for up to 3 months.

DULCE DE LECHE CHEESECAKE WITH GUAVA SAUCE

If you've never made a cheesecake, this is the one to start with (and if you have, you should try this one)! The texture is reminiscent of a traditional Italian ricotta cheesecake: It's light, silky soft, and not overly sweet. Sonora patrons—and my relatives—always ask me to make cheesecakes for their parties. The guava sauce adds a nice finishing touch of flavor and color. Serve this at room temperature with a cup of good Colombian coffee. MAKES TWO 9-INCH CAKES

42 ounces Dulce de Leche (page 178)

24 ounces cream cheese at room temperature

1 cup heavy cream

4 eggs

Guava Sauce:

3/4 cup guava purée

1/4 cup water

Preheat the oven to 350°F. Position a rack in the center of the oven.

In the bowl of an electric mixer, combine the dulce de leche and cream cheese. Beat until well blended. Beat in the heavy cream and eggs until completely smooth. Scrape the batter into two 9-inch springform pans. Place the pans in a roasting pan, and fill the roasting pan with water to come halfway up the side of the spring-form pan. Place the roasting pan in oven and bake for 70 minutes, or until a knife inserted in the center of the cake comes out clean. The top will be dry and browned.

Remove from the oven and the roasting pan. Let cool on a wire rack for at least 1 hour. Cover and refrigerate at least 2 hours, or up to 2 weeks. Run a knife around the edge of each pan, place the pan on a plate, and remove the sides.

To make the sauce: In a small bowl, mix the guava purée and water. Put the sauce in a squeeze bottle and drizzle it over the cheesecake or make decorative dots of sauce on the serving plate or platter.

DRINKS

COLOMBIAN FRUIT PUNCH (SALPICÓN DE FRUTAS)

I can't remember going to a Colombian fiesta where this refreshing fruit punch wasn't served! *Salpicón*, which literally means "hodgepodge," gets its name from the fabulous mixture of tropical fruits—mangos, pineapple, and watermelon, just to name a few—found in this punch. Usually it's served in large colorful ceramic bowls and scooped into glasses. Because it's so packed with fruit, we serve it with a spoon. Feel free to vary the fruit combinations according to taste and availability. SERVES 12

1 small watermelon, peeled, seeded, and cut into small chunks

1 bunch red or green seedless grapes, sliced or cut into quarters

1 pineapple, peeled, cored, and cut into $1/4$-inch chunks

2 mangos, peeled, cut from pit, and finely diced

2 to 3 pears, peeled, cored, and finely diced

2 to 3 apples, peeled, cored, and finely diced

6 cups Colombiana (Colombian soda) or orange soda

In a punch bowl, combine all the fruit. Pour the soda over and stir once. Serve immediately, in glasses. To prepare ahead of time, cut up all the fruit except the apples and store in an airtight container in the refrigerator for up to 2 days. Add the apple and the liquid just before serving.

CAIPIRINHA

Spring not only brings daffodils and birds to Manhattan, it also brings caipirinha fans to the out-door café at Sonora. Brazil's national cocktail will make your guests want to dance the samba all night long. Cachaça, the main ingredient in this cocktail, is quite powerful; Brazilians claim it will not only enhance your mood, but also help you to speak Portuguese! SERVES 1

2 limes, scrubbed and cut into 6 wedges

2 teaspoons superfine sugar

2 ounces ($1/4$ cup) cachaça (Brazilian rum)

Ice cubes

Put the lime wedges in a cocktail shaker and add the sugar. Use a pestle or the end of a wooden spoon to mash limes and sugar together. Add the cachaça and several ice cubes. Shake well and strain into a glass filled with ice.

MORA CAIPIRINHA

The tartness of the lime blends beautifully with the fragrant *mora* to create a wonderful variation on the classic Brazilian caipirinha. SERVES 1

1/2 cup thawed frozen *mora* pulp

1/4 cup water

3 tablespoons superfine sugar

1 lime, cut into 4 wedges

2 ounces (1/4 cup) cachaça (Brazilian rum)

Ice cubes

In a glass, combine the *mora*, water, and 2 tablespoons of the sugar. Stir to dissolve the sugar. In a cocktail shaker, combine the lime wedges and remaining 1 tablespoon sugar. Using a pestle or the end of a wooden spoon, mash the lime pieces to extract the juice and oil from the skin. Add the cachaça and the *mora* mixture. Cover and shake briskly. Pour into a glass of ice and serve immediately.

CUBAN MINT COCKTAIL (MOJITO DE MENTA)

Mojito comes from the Spanish word *mojar*, which means "to wet." This classic Cuban cocktail is aptly named: It's incredibly thirst-quenching! SERVES 1

- 10 fresh mint leaves, plus 1 sprig for garnish
- Juice from 2 limes
- 1/3 cup water
- 2 tablespoons superfine sugar, or to taste
- 1 cup crushed ice
- 1 1/2 ounces light rum
- Sprite or 7-Up for topping off

Tear the mint leaves in half and put in a cocktail shaker. Using a pestle or the end of a wooden spoon, mash the leaves until bruised and crushed. Add all the remaining ingredients except soda. Cover the shaker and shake briskly. Pour into a tall glass and top off with Sprite or 7-Up. Stir once, garnish with the mint sprig, and serve.

COLOMBIAN BEER COOLER (REFAJO COLOMBIANO)

Die-hard beer fans may balk at what at first seems sacrilegious (diluting beer!), but I promise you that there is nothing like a *refajo* to cool down a steamy day or a chipotle-sparked dish. MAKES 1 SERVING

6 ounces (1/2 bottle) Aguila beer or any type of lager

6 ounces Colombiana (Colombian soda) or orange soda

Pour the beer into a chilled glass. Pour in the soda and serve immediately.

RASPBERRY MIMOSA (MIMOSA DE FRAMBUESA)

Light and refreshing, this mimosa is as welcome at a wintry midday brunch as it is on a sultry summer evening. MAKES 6 DRINKS

1 cup fresh raspberries

1 ounce (2 tablespoons) raspberry liqueur (Chambord)

1 bottle chilled Spanish sparkling wine or good-quality Champagne

Reserve 18 of the raspberries for garnish. Put the remaining raspberries into a cock-tail shaker or a small bowl. Add the raspberry liqueur. Using a pestle or the back of a wooden spoon, smash the berries and liqueur together into a paste. Evenly distribute the mixture among 6 Champagne glasses. Pour the chilled wine or Champagne into the glasses. Top each drink with 3 raspberries and serve immediately.

MANGO AND LEMONGRASS SANGRÍA

There is nothing like an outdoor summertime party. Picnic tables dressed in multicolored table-cloths look that much more beautiful with fruit-filled brimming pitchers of sangría next to platters of wonderful treats for your guests. This sangría is a tropical version of the Spanish classic. If you can get your hands on fresh lemongrass (available in most Thai and Indian markets, as well as by mail order), it makes a wonderful garnish for this refreshing drink. Cut all your fruit (with the exception of the apple, because it will brown) the morning of the party and store in the refrigerator in a covered container. You can also prepare the sangría ahead of time to keep last-minute work to a minimum. The nonalcoholic version of this sangría is also *fabulosa!* SERVES 4 TO 6

1 cup mango nectar

1 1/2 cups dry white wine

1 cup pineapple juice

4 ounces (1/2 cup) Triple Sec

1 apple, cored and cut into 1/2-inch chunks

1 mango, peeled, cut from pit, and finely diced

Ice cubes

1 stalk lemongrass, peeled and cut into 4 to 6 thin lengthwise slices, for garnish

1 orange, sliced crosswise and then into half-moons, for garnish

In a large pitcher, combine the mango nectar, wine, pineapple juice, Triple Sec, apple, and mango. Add the ice cubes, stir well, and pour into wineglasses. Garnish with lemongrass and orange slices.

PASSION FRUIT MARGARITA

Passion fruit *(maracuyá)*, a Brazilian native, has a distinctive sweet-tart flavor that adds depth to sauces and drinks. Currently grown in New Zealand, Australia, California, Florida, and Hawaii (where it's called *lilikoi*), the aromatic passion fruit can be found in Latin-American groceries and supermarkets. Here, the seductive taste of passion fruit is combined with the wonderfully woody flavor of Tres Generaciones Sauza gold tequila. The results, as I am sure you and your guests will agree, are wonderful. SERVES 2

4 ounces ($\frac{1}{2}$ cup) thawed frozen passion fruit purée

2 tablespoons confectioners' sugar or to taste

4 ounces ($\frac{1}{2}$ cup) Tres Generaciones Sauza Tequila or other gold tequila

$\frac{1}{4}$ cup fresh lime juice

1 ounce (2 tablespoons) Triple Sec

Ice cubes

In a glass, combine the passion fruit purée with the sugar and stir to dissolve the sugar. Add the tequila, lime juice, and Triple Sec. Stir. Pour into a cocktail shaker filled with ice, cover, and shake. Pour into 2 balloon wineglasses and serve immediately.

MORA MARGARITA

This drink was born on a fun-filled sultry summer afternoon. While my wife, Martha, and I were waiting for our guests to arrive, we came up with a Colombian interpretation of a Mexican classic. In this version, the Grand Marnier complements the margarita by releasing the sweet summery flavor of the *mora*, or South American blackberry, available as frozen pulp in many Latin-American groceries. If you can't find it, frozen raspberries will do just fine. MAKES 4 DRINKS

1 cup thawed frozen *mora* purée or puréed thawed frozen unsweetened raspberries

2½ tablespoons confectioners' sugar

8 ounces (1 cup) Grand Marnier or other orange liqueur

½ cup fresh lime juice

6 ounces (3/4 cup) tequila

Ice cubes

Lime slices for garnish

In a blender, combine all the ingredients except the ice and lime slices. Process until smooth. Divide among 4 ice-filled glasses. Garnish with lime slices and serve immediately.

MANGO MARTINI

My friend Brendan absolutely loves martinis but is not too crazy about tropical cocktails. In an effort to win him over, I devised this mango martini. Not only did Brendan like it, so did my guests at Sonora. This very simple drink packs a wallop, so don't be deceived by the sweetness of the mango! SERVES 4

Ice cubes

6 ounces (3/4 cup) gin

8 ounces (1 cup) mango nectar, chilled

In a shaker filled with ice, combine the gin and nectar. Shake well and pour into chilled martini glasses. Serve immediately.

TEQUILA COCKTAIL, MEXICAN STYLE (SANGRITA)

Recently, I had the pleasure of being initiated into the world of *sangrita*, and my tequila drinking hasn't been the same since! On a sunny Saturday afternoon in the lovely market of San Angel, just outside Mexico City, I enjoyed a fabulous fresh taco lunch, an exciting conversation with an old friend, and some of the best tequila I've ever had. Only it wasn't just the tequila that was so wonderful, it was the *sangrita*, the little drink that was served with it. This tasty liquid is deep red in color, hence the name, which literally means "little blood." It's usually served in a shot glass along with the tequila. As my dear friend Adriana taught me, *sangrita* should be sipped along with the tequila. Some people, she claims, actually hold the *sangrita* in their mouths, take a sip of the tequila, and let the two drinks blend together before swallowing. Others pour their *sangrita* into their favorite tequila (you'll need a larger glass in order to do this) to make what Mexicans call a *vampiro*, or vampire. *Sangrita* makes a great party drink—some even enjoy it without the tequila! MAKES 4 SHOTS

1 1/2 tablespoons fresh lemon juice

1 tablespoon grenadine

2 dashes Worcestershire sauce

2 dashes Tabasco sauce

1 cup plus 2 tablespoons tomato juice

3 tablespoons fresh orange juice

Kosher salt to taste, plus more for dipping

Freshly ground pepper to taste

Using your finger, moisten the rims of 4 shot glasses with a little of the lemon juice. In a cocktail shaker, combine the remaining lemon juice, the grenadine, Worcestershire sauce, Tabasco sauce, tomato juice, orange juice, salt, and pepper. Shake to blend. Turn the shot glasses upside down onto a plate of kosher salt. Pour the *sangrita* into the shot glasses and line them up next to shots of your favorite tequila. (You can prepare the *sangrita* ahead of time, and store it in a covered container in the refrigerator for up to 5 days.)

RUM AND COCA-COLA (CUBA LIBRE)

This mambo-inspiring drink is my favorite version of an old-time classic. SERVES 1

3 ounces (1/3 cup) dark rum

Ice cubes

2 tablespoons (1 ounce) gin

4 drops angostura bitters

6 ounces Coca-Cola

1 lime, cut into quarters, plus 1 slice for garnish

Pour the rum into a glass filled with ice. Add the gin and bitters. Fill the rest of the glass with Coca-Cola. Squeeze the lime quarters over. Stir, garnish with the lime slice, and serve.

MORA AND AGUARDIENTE COCKTAIL (AMOR ARDIENTE)

The flavor of *mora*, intensely flavored dark purple South American berries, reminds me of Siete de Agosto, a huge market in Bogotá, Colombia. My mother would take my sister, brother, and me along when she went there to buy food for our weekend dinners. She would give us our allowance, and we'd immediately go to buy ourselves a treat: a *batida*, or fresh fruit juice, made from *mora*. In this cocktail, the tartness of the blackberry is beautifully balanced by the aguardiente and sugar. Though it could be served any time of year, this colorful cocktail is an ideal summertime or early-fall treat. SERVES 1

1 cup crushed ice

1½ ounces (3 tablespoons) aguardiente (Colombian brandy) or Greek ouzo

½ cup thawed frozen unsweetened *mora* purée (found in Latin-American markets),
   or puréed thawed frozen unsweetened raspberries

¼ cup water

3 tablespoons superfine sugar, or to taste

1 mint sprig for garnish

Fill a shaker with the ice. In a glass, combine the aguardiente or ouzo, the *mora* or raspberries, water, and sugar. Stir well and pour into the shaker. Cover and shake briskly. Pour into a glass, garnish with the mint sprig, and serve immediately.

SOUTH AMERICAN EGGNOG (SABAJÓN)

This decadently rich drink is a classic Colombian Christmastime cocktail. It's so luscious that it could stand alone as a dessert. SERVES 1

1 ounce (2 tablespoons) aguardiente (Colombian brandy) or Greek ouzo

1/4 cup Dulce de Leche (page 178)

1 tablespoon Kahlúa or other coffee liqueur

1 ounce (2 tablespoons) brandy

1 cup crushed ice

1 cinnamon stick for garnish

In a blender, combine the aguardiente or ouzo, dulce de leche, Kahlúa, and brandy. Blend until smooth. Pour over ice and serve with a cinnamon stick.

LATIN-AMERICAN HOT TODDY (CANELAZOS)

Just a fleeting whiff of this comforting cocktail brings back memories of cool Colombian mountain air. *Panela*, sold in one-pound loaves in Latin-American markets, blends beautifully with the aguardiente (Colombian brandy). Try this Latin-American variation of a classic New England drink to remove the chill of a crisp fall day. SERVES 2

3¹/₂ cups water

¹/₂ loaf *panela* or ¹/₂ cup packed light brown sugar

2 ounces (¹/₄ cup) aguardiente (Colombian brandy)

1 tablespoon ground cinnamon

2 lime wedges for garnish

In a medium saucepan, bring the water to a simmer, add the *panela* or brown sugar and aguardiente, and stir until the sugar is dissolved. Stir in the cinnamon. Bring the mixture just to a simmer and pour into 2 mugs. Serve hot, with a lime wedge.

BASICS

Just as any tall building needs a solid foundation, each cuisine has its key building blocks. For my brand of nuevo Latino cooking, which incorporates the flavors of Colombia and other Latin-American cuisines and the techniques of my French culinary education, these recipes and techniques are fundamental both in my kitchen at home and in my restaurant.

CHIPOTLE PURÉE

Empty a can of *chipotles en adobo* into a blender or food processor and blend until smooth. Cover and store in the refrigerator for up to 6 months. One 13 1/2-ounce can of *chipotles en adobo* makes about 10 ounces chipotle purée.

CHIPOTLE MAYONNAISE

Combine 1 cup mayonnaise with 1 tablespoon chipotle purée. Cover and refrigerate for up to 2 days. Makes 1 cup.

BLACK BEANS (FRIJOLES NEGROS)

Though we Latinos are different in many ways, we do share one common culinary characteristic: beans. Great in many kinds of dishes, black beans are hearty and tasty enough to stand alone.

SERVES 12

1 pound dried black beans

6 to 8 cups chicken stock (page 180), canned low-salt chicken broth, or water

1 green plantain, peeled (page 194) and cut into 1/2-inch chunks (optional)

Kosher salt to taste

Chopped fresh cilantro for garnish

Rinse and pick over the beans. Put them in a stockpot and add broth, stock, or water to cover by 2 inches. Bring to a simmer, cover, and cook for 1 1/2 to 2 hours, or until tender but not mushy. Add the plantain, if desired, after 1 hour and 15 minutes. (Remove the plantain prior to serving or freezing.) Add the salt at the end of cooking time. Garnish with cilantro. Serve now, or let cool, cover, and refrigerate for up to 5 days or freeze for up to 3 months.

BLANCHED OCTOPUS

Unlike their Latin-American counterparts, I've found that many people in the States are reluctant to eat this delicious eight-tentacled sea creature. In spite of that, I am proud to say that I have converted many a wary octopus-eater by first serving them *pulpo* dishes (such as octopus ceviche, page 60) and then announcing the ingredients. Though octopus can be tough unless prepared correctly, it is easily tenderized by blanching. I promise you that you'll discover why so many Latin Americans enjoy *pulpo*'s enriching flavor in soups, stews, and ceviches. As far as cooking methods go, I think this one yields the most tender octopus, though an Italian friend swears that adding corks to the cooking water helps make it even more succulent!

12 cups water

1 teaspoon kosher salt

1 bay leaf

1 onion, quartered

6 cloves garlic

6 peppercorns

1 fresh or thawed frozen octopus (about 2 pounds), cleaned (ask your fish market to do this)

In a stockpot over high heat, combine the water, salt, bay leaf, onion, garlic, and peppercorns. Bring to a boil. Using tongs, dunk the octopus in the boiling water for about 5 seconds. Hold it up for a moment, then repeat (this process helps to increase tenderness). Put the octopus back in the liquid, cover, and simmer for about 1 hour.

(Test for tenderness by trying a small piece. If it's not tender, continue cooking and checking every 15 minutes.)

Remove the pot from heat and let the octopus sit in the hot liquid for 60 minutes. Drain and let cool completely, then remove the loose skin. Use now, or cover tightly and refrigerate for up to 5 days.

DULCE DE LECHE

Dulce de leche, also known as *arequipe* in Colombia, or *manjar blanco* or *cajeta* throughout Latin America, is wooing new fans in the United States. This silky-smooth caramel has been gracing cookies, cakes, and all kinds of tasty treats for many years in Latin America, long before Häagen Dazs introduced its Dulce de Leche ice cream. *Dulce de leche* is a key ingredient in Sofia's Dulce de Leche Oatmeal Cookies (page 147), as well as in many other dessert recipes. But you will also enjoy it, as my kids do, slightly warmed and served over vanilla ice cream or even fresh fruit. Here are two recipes: one is the one my *abuelita* used, and the other is a less-labor-intensive method. Generally, I choose the latter, and boil several cans at a time.

GRANDMA'S RECIPE (LA RECETA DE ABUELITA)

- 1 quart whole milk
- 2 cups sugar
- 1/4 teaspoon baking soda
- Pinch of ground cinnamon

In a large saucepan, combine all ingredients and cook over medium heat, without stirring, for 15 to 20 minutes. Reduce heat to low and cook, stirring constantly with a wooden spoon, for 25 to 30 minutes, or until it thickens so much that you can see the bottom of the pan as you stir. Remove from heat and let cool. Cover and refrigerate it for up to 2 weeks. You may need to heat it slightly in order to soften it before using. MAKES ABOUT I 3/4 CUPS

EASY DULCE DE LECHE

Put one 14-ounce can sweetened condensed milk in a stockpot and add cold water to cover. Bring the water to a boil and let boil for 1 hour and 45 minutes. Check the water level frequently to make sure it is always covering the can. Do not boil for more than 2 hours, or you will overcook the *dulce de leche* and run the risk of exploding the can (which, I am happy to report, has never happened to me, though we have been using this method in my family for many, many years). Using tongs, occasionally turn the can to stir the milk.

Remove the can from the water and let cool to room temperature. Transfer the caramelized milk to an airtight container, cover, and store in the refrigerator for up to 2 weeks. MAKES I 3/4 CUPS

CHICKEN STOCK (CALDO DE POLLO)

A tasty chicken stock is the secret to many wonderful Latin-American dishes, ranging from stews to rice. MAKES ABOUT 6 CUPS

1 small chicken (about 3½ pounds), quartered

2½ quarts cold water

1 teaspoon kosher salt

1 large celery stalk with leaves, coarsely chopped

2 carrots, peeled and coarsely chopped

1 onion, coarsely chopped

1 bay leaf

1 bunch cilantro, stemmed and coarsely chopped

Clove from 1 small head garlic

Rinse the chicken well and trim off all excess fat. Put it in a large stockpot and add water. Add the salt and bring to a boil. Skim off any fat or scum that rises to the surface. Add the remaining ingredients and reduce heat to low. Simmer until the chicken is fork-tender, about 2 hours, skimming occasionally as necessary. Add water as needed to keep the chicken covered.

Pour the stock through a fine-mesh sieve into another pot or a large bowl, pressing on solids with the back of a large spoon to release the liquid. Spoon off the fat that rises to the top. You can make the stock even clearer by straining it through paper towels. Let cool to room temperature. Transfer to airtight containers and refrigerate overnight. Remove the congealed fat from the stock. Store in the refrigerator for up to 3 days, or freeze for up to 3 months.

FISH STOCK (CALDO DE PESCADO)

A great fish stock is the secret of success for many Latin-American fish dishes, soups, and stews. Get to know the folks in your local fish market so that they can make suggestions and provide you with fish bones. You'll find that the more varied your fish is, the richer your stock will be. Although this recipe uses snapper, my personal favorite for stock, you can use any mild-flavored white-fleshed fish, such as cod, cusk, flounder, grouper, hake, halibut, or sea bass. You can also make a shrimp or lobster stock using their shells; freeze them to use in the future. MAKES ABOUT 8 CUPS

2 tablespoons extra-virgin olive oil

2 red onions, coarsely chopped

2 plum tomatoes, diced

1 bay leaf

1 large celery stalk with leaves, coarsely chopped

1 bunch cilantro, stemmed

Clove from 1 head garlic

1/2 cup brandy

1 bottle dry white wine such as Pinot Grigio

3 quarts cold water

3 pounds fish bones, scraps, or heads (from red snapper, or another mild, white-fleshed fish), rinsed

2 teaspoons kosher salt

(continued)

In a stockpot, heat the oil over medium heat. Add the onions, tomatoes, bay leaf, celery, cilantro, and garlic. Cook, stirring, until soft, 5 to 8 minutes. Add the brandy and stir. Add the wine, water, fish bones, and salt. Bring to a boil, reduce heat to medium, and simmer for about 45 minutes (if you cook the bones too long, the stock will become bitter), skimming off any foam as necessary.

Pour the stock through a fine-mesh sieve lined with paper towels into another pot or large bowl, pressing on the solids with the back of a large spoon. Let cool to room temperature. Transfer to airtight containers and refrigerate for up to 2 days, or freeze for up to 2 months.

GARLIC OIL

This oil is absolutely indispensable in my kitchen. I use it for everything from marinating shrimp to salad dressings. And I have been known to drizzle it on toasted Italian bread—after all, garlic does have a myriad of curative powers.

1 tablespoon roasted garlic (page 184)

1 cup canola oil

Kosher salt and freshly ground pepper to taste

In a blender or food processor, purée the garlic. With the machine running, gradually add the oil and process just until mixed. Add salt and pepper. Use now, or cover tightly and refrigerate for up to 3 days. Mix well before serving.

ROASTED VEGETABLES

ROASTED CORN:

Peel back the husks and remove the corn silk. Fold the husks back over the corn, place the ear on an oven rack, and roast, rotating every few minutes, in a preheated 375°F oven for 15 to 20 minutes. If using fresh or thawed corn kernels, toss them in olive oil with a bit of garlic in a very hot skillet until lightly browned.

ROASTED GARLIC:

For single cloves of garlic: Peel, place on a square of aluminum foil, sprinkle with kosher salt, and wrap in the foil. Roast in a preheated 350°F oven for 12 to 15 minutes. For a whole head of garlic: Remove the loose skin, wrap the garlic in aluminum foil, and roast in a preheated 350°F oven for 45 to 60 minutes, or until very tender. To remove, squeeze the pulp out of the skin.

ROASTED TOMATOES:

Core the tomatoes and halve them lengthwise. Place on a broiler pan or baking sheet, cut-side down. Roast under a preheated broiler, as close to the heat source as possible, for 6 to 8 minutes, or until browned and blistered all over. Peel off the skin. Don't worry if it doesn't all come off; charred skin adds great flavor. Or, roast whole tomatoes on an oiled grill or in an oiled grill pan for 8 to 10 minutes, turning them periodically with tongs.

ROASTED ONIONS:

Remove the outer, dry skin. Rub the onions with a light coat of olive oil, place on a baking sheet, and sprinkle with kosher salt. Roast in a preheated 350°F oven for about 45 minutes.

ROASTED AND PEELED PEPPERS AND CHILIES:

Spike a whole pepper with a long fork and hold it directly over a gas flame (or place on a grill over hot coals, or in a very hot cast-iron skillet), turning the pepper so that it becomes charred on all sides. Place in a plastic or paper bag and close the bag. Let sit for about 10 minutes, or until cool to the touch. Pull out the stem and rub off the black skin. Cut the pepper in half and remove the seeds with your hands—don't use water or you will lose those wonderful oils you worked so hard to get! Use right away, or submerge in olive oil, cover tightly, and refrigerate for up to 3 days.

To roast peppers under a broiler: Cut the peppers in half lengthwise. Core them and remove the seeds and ribs. Lay the peppers, skin-side up, on a baking sheet close to the heat source of a preheated broiler and broil until the skins are charred. Chilies can be roasted and peeled in the same ways.

COOKED YUCA

Like many Latin Americans, I grew up with this potatolike vegetable, which is served in a variety of soups, stews, salads—and fried, as a side dish with fabulous sauces. (Yuca pastel and yuca fries are two very popular side dishes at Sonora.) In the United States this tuber has gone from the obscure to the highly visible in a relatively short period of time. Cooking the yuca in stock or broth brings out its nutty, buttery flavor. I recommend buying frozen yuca (available in the freezer sections of most large supermarkets), simply because then you don't have to peel it, but frozen yuca is not as sturdy as fresh. If you choose to buy it fresh (look for it in the produce section of most large supermarkets), follow the directions below.

To peel fresh *yuca*: Cover a work surface with a kitchen towel (yuca is quite starchy and will leave a white residue). Stand the yuca on end and, using a sharp knife, slice it lengthwise. Use a heavier knife to cut the yuca into 3-inch sections.

Put the yuca in a stockpot and add stock, broth, or water to cover by 2 inches. Bring to a boil, reduce heat, and simmer, uncovered, for about 25 minutes, or until tender. Using a slotted spoon, transfer to paper towels to drain and let cool to the touch. (If not using the yuca right away, let it cool in the liquid in which it was cooked.) Cut the sections in half lengthwise and remove the stringy core that runs down the center either by pulling with your fingers or using a sharp knife. Cover and refrigerate for up to 3 days.

SAZÓN SPICE BLEND

Sazón spice blend is a cumin-and-garlic blend that is sold throughout the United States in both large and small supermarkets. The Goya blend uses monosodium glutamate, so here's a homemade version. MAKES ABOUT 3 TABLESPOONS

1 teaspoon annatto powder (ground achiote seeds)

$^1/_2$ teaspoon dried cilantro leaves

2 teaspoons garlic powder

2 teaspoons ground cumin

1 teaspoon freshly ground pepper

3 teaspoons kosher salt

In a small bowl, mix all the ingredients together. Store in an airtight container for up to 6 months.

SOURCES

Though most ingredients in this book are available in supermarkets, these sources offer a convenient way for you to order them. Besides, it's great fun to look through the catalogs and Web sites—you'll find all kinds of goodies to add to your pantry.

Dean and DeLuca
Catalog Department
560 Broadway
New York, NY 10012
Phone: (800) 221-7714
Web site: www.deandeluca.com
Chilies, dried beans, annatto seeds, masa harina, spices.

D'Artagnan
280 Wilson Avenue
Newark, NJ 07105
Phone: (800) 327-8246
Fax: (973) 465-1870
Web site: www.dartagnan.com
Organic game, poultry, exotic specialties.

Frieda's
4465 Corporate Center Drive
Los Alamitos, CA 90720
Phone: (800) 241-1771
Web site: www.friedas.com
A wide variety of produce, corn husks, banana leaves, and more.

Melissa's/World Variety Produce
P.O. Box 21127
Los Angeles, CA 90021
Phone: (800) 588-0151
Web site: www.melissas.com
Fresh and dried Latin American produce, chilies, and grains.

Mo Hotta Mo Betta
P.O. Box 4136
San Luis Obispo, CA 93403
Phone: (800) 462-3220
Web site: www.mohotta.com
Hot sauces, spices, chilies, annatto seeds, and more.

Penzey's Spices
Muskego, WI
Phone: (800) 741-7787
Fax: (262) 679-7878
Web site: www.penzeys.com
A wide variety of spices.

Tropic-Good Distributors
33–60 55th Street
Woodside, NY 11377
Phone: (718) 533-7181
A variety of Latin-American ingredients.

Williams Sonoma
Phone: (800) 840-2591
Web site: www.williams-sonoma.com
*A variety of spices, imported products, kitchen
equipment, and more.*

INGREDIENT GLOSSARY

Though many of these items may already be *conocidos*, or known to you, others will probably be new. Here is a brief description of some of the most important ingredients in my style of Latin-American cooking. (Some Spanish vegetable or fruit names will vary, depending on the region.)

Achiote seeds (see annatto powder)

Aguardiente (ah-gwahr-DIEN-tay), Colombia's national liquor, is an anise-flavored brandy made from sugarcane syrup. It can usually be found in large liquor stores. The Greek liquor ouzo is an acceptable substitute.

Aguila is an amber-colored, full-bodied Colombian beer that can be found throughout the United States in supermarkets.

Ají (ah-HEE) is one of the Spanish names for chili pepper.

Ají amarillo (ah-HEE ah-mah-REE-yo), yellow chili, is a spicy chili used throughout Peru to flavor many dishes (such as Ají de Gallina, page 124, and Papas a la Huancaína, page 77). It can be found in Latin-American markets (or through mail order) in a dried powdered or paste form.

Ají mirasol (ah-HEE mee-rah-SOLE) is similar to *ají amarillo*, but darker in color and milder in flavor.

Annatto powder is made from ground achiote seeds, native to Central America and the Caribbean. The rust-colored powder, used throughout Latin America, adds a natural coloring and earthy flavor to all kinds of dishes, both sweet and savory.

Arequipe (ah-ray-KEE-pay) is the Colombian name for *dulce de leche,* or caramelized milk.

Cachaça (kah-CHAH-sa), Brazil's national liquor and the main ingredient in the famous Brazilian cocktail caipirinha, is rum made from sugarcane. Light rum can be used as a substitute.

Ceviche (say-VEE-chay), a dish indigenous to Peru, can be found in many parts of Latin America. It is typically made of fish that is marinated, or "cooked," by the acidic juices of citrus fruits, usually limes.

Chorizo (chor-EE-soh), a pork sausage, is used in many Latin-American dishes. I prefer the Colombian chorizo, either fresh or dried, which is both lighter and less *picante* (spicy) than its Mexican counterpart. If you can't find dried Colombian chorizo, use Mexican chorizo or sweet Italian sausage sautéed with a pinch of achiote.

Chipotle (chee-POHT-lay) chilies are ripened and smoked jalapeño chilies. These Mexican chilies, which are fiery hot, enhance many dishes with their fabulous smoky flavor. Chipotles are most often found in cans *(chipotles en adobo)* in Mexican and other Latin-American markets, preserved in a vinegar and tomato sauce.

Colombiana is a fruity-flavored Colombian soda found at many Latin-American markets.

Dos Equis is a Mexican beer widely available in the States.

Empanadas (em-pah-NAH-dahs) are stuffed half-moon pastry turnovers found throughout Latin America. Empanada leaves, which can be used in place of making the homemade dough, can be found frozen (Goya brand) in many supermarkets.

Guajillo (gwah-HEE-yo), a spicy dried chili found in many Latin-American markets, has a shiny brownish-red skin and a fruity, citrusy flavor.

Guava (GWAH-vah), a sweet and fragrant tropical fruit from South America, is now grown in California, Florida, and Hawaii. This oval-shaped fruit is usually about 2 inches in diameter. Its skin ranges in color from yellow to purple-black, and the flesh varies in color from light yellow to bright red. Though it's not common to find fresh guava unless you live in a region where they're grown, guava paste, jelly, marmalade, and frozen guava purée can be found in Latin-American markets and many supermarkets all around the United States.

Harina precocida (ah-REE-nah pray-koh-SEE-dah), also called *masarepa* (mah-sah-RAY-pah), is pre-cooked cornmeal used to make Colombian corncakes (*arepas*) and empanadas. This cornmeal, which is substantially more elastic than other cornmeals, can be found in Latin-American markets, or through mail order. I use the Venezolana brand.

Malanga (mah-LAHN-gah), also known as *yautía*, is a tropical tuber with a rough, barklike skin. Its shape sometime resembles that of a knotty carrot or a turnip. It can be found in Caribbean and Latin-American markets. The variety I usually find in New York has a bright ivory flesh with what looks like little brown threads running through it. Store at room temperature for up to 1 week, or peel, dice, and freeze for future use. This potatolike vegetable, which should be firm with no moldy or soft spots, can be boiled, steamed, or stewed.

Mango, a delectable fruit found throughout Latin America (and now cultivated in California and Florida), is originally from India, where the mango tree is considered sacred. Mangos vary in shape (round, oblong, and kidney) and weight (from 6 ounces to about 4 pounds). Their thin but tough skin changes from green to yellow and red when ripe. The fragrant orange mango flesh must be carefully cut away from its large seed with a sharp knife. I use the fresh fruit, the nectar (preferably Mira brand), and dried mango (sold in chunks and strips in natural foods stores, gourmet markets, and by mail order) in a number of dishes.

Mora (MOR-ah), a South-American blackberry, is sold as pulp (unsweetened frozen purée) in many Latin-American markets. Puréed unsweetened frozen raspberries are an acceptable substitute.

Panela (pah-NAY-lah), also called *piloncillo* (pee-lon-SEE-yo), is a tropical hardened brown cane sugar sold in loaves throughout much of Latin America. Though *panela* can be found in Latin-American markets (and ordered—see page 188), dark or light brown sugar can be used as a substitute.

Passion fruit, sometimes called *maracuyá* (ma-ra-koo-YAH) or *granadilla* (grah-nah-DEE-ya) in Spanish, was named *pasiflora* by missionaries who compared the different parts of the plant's flower to symbols of Christ's crucifixion, such as the crown of thorns. A native of Brazil, this tropical fruit is about the size of a plum. Its skin, which is dimpled and purplish or yellow in color, protects an incredibly fragrant interior of soft flesh filled with tiny edible black seeds. Unsweetened frozen passion fruit pulp (purée) can be found in many Latin-American groceries, or by mail order.

Pasteles (pah-STAY-less), depending where you are in Latin America, can be empanadas or tamales, and can be either savory or sweet. I use *pasteles* to refer to dough-crusted savory meat-stuffed rolls.

Peruvian olives, *aceitunas de botija* (ah-say-TOO-nahs day bo-TEE-hah), are large black, juicy olives. Kalamata olives can be substituted, but they are not as moist as their Peruvian counterparts.

Plantains, or *plátanos* (PLAH-tah-nos), have a long and rich history in Latin-American cooking. Eaten at all stages of ripeness—from unripe green to yellow to brown to fully ripe black—these "cooking bananas," which look like overgrown bananas, can now be found in most large supermarkets. Unlike the banana, they are inedible unless cooked.

All plantains can be baked, boiled, and fried. Green plantains are used like potatoes in many recipes and are an integral part of many Latin-American soups. They are also ideal for frying to make *tostones*, coin-shaped plantain chips. Sweet plantains can be boiled and mashed with potatoes to make *naco*, or mashed potatoes. Green plantains can be hard to peel, so soak them in warm water for 15 to 20 minutes, then cut a slit lengthwise down the plantain and open the skin by peeling it back (or use a knife to peel the skin). Riper plantains can usually be peeled like bananas.

Pommery mustard is a sharp, grainy mustard with an intense flavor. This mustard can be found in supermarkets around the United States, or through mail-order companies. Dijon mustard is an acceptable substitute.

Sazón (sah-ZOHN) means "taste," or "flavor," in Spanish. It is also a spice blend made of cumin and garlic. Though it is sold in supermarkets all over the United States, it is easy to make a home-made version (see page 187).

Tequila (tay-KEE-lah) is the name of a town located thirty miles west of Guadalajara, Mexico, and also the name of the famous liquor made by fermenting and distilling the sap of the agave plant *(Agave tequilana)*. Mexico produces hundreds of tequilas, which vary in both strength and color (depending on the fermentation). I usually use Tres Generaciones, an *añejo*, or gold tequila.

Terra Chips, a brand name of all-natural vegetable chips, can be found in large supermarkets throughout the United States.

Tiradito (tee-RAH-dee-TOH) is the name of a Peruvian dish that resembles Italian carpaccio and Japanese sashimi. *Tiraditos*, which can be made of thin slices of raw meat or fish, are usually served with light sauces drizzled on top.

Tostones (toes-TONE-ace) are Colombian chips made of coin-shaped fried green plantains. The green plantains are thinly sliced, and then lightly pounded prior to frying.

Yuca (YOO-kah), also called *manioc,* looks like a long, thick root (usually between 6 and 20 inches in length, and about 2 to 3 inches in diameter) covered in a smooth (often waxed) dark brown, bark-like skin, which is peeled to reveal a crisp white flesh. This root is used to make tapioca as well as flour, and is used in a number of Brazilian and Caribbean dishes.

INDEX

TABLE OF EQUIVALENTS

The exact equivalents in the following tables have been rounded for convenience.

LIQUID/DRY MEASURES

U.S.	METRIC
1/4 teaspoon	1.25 milliliters
1/2 teaspoon	2.5 milliliters
1 teaspoon	5 milliliters
1 tablespoon (3 teaspoons)	15 milliliters
1 fluid ounce (2 tablespoons)	30 milliliters
1/4 cup	60 milliliters
1/3 cup	80 milliliters
1/2 cup	120 milliliters
1 cup	240 milliliters
1 pint (2 cups)	480 milliliters
1 quart (4 cups, 32 ounces)	960 milliliters
1 gallon (4 quarts)	3.84 liters
1 ounce (by weight)	28 grams
1 pound	454 grams
2.2 pounds	1 kilogram

LENGTH

U.S.	METRIC
1/8 inch	3 millimeters
1/4 inch	6 millimeters
1/2 inch	12 millimeters
1 inch	2.5 centimeters

OVEN TEMPERATURE

FAHRENHEIT	CELSIUS	GAS
250	120	1/2
275	140	1
300	150	2
325	160	3
350	180	4
375	190	5
400	200	6
425	220	7
450	230	8
475	240	9
500	260	10